HARCOURT SOCIAL Studies

The United States:
MAKING A NEW NATION

Homework and Practice Book
Teacher Edition

D1198443

 Harcourt
SCHOOL PUBLISHERS

www.harcourtschool.com

Printed in the United States of America

ISBN-13: 978-0-15-347303-6

16 1838 18 17

4500660825   B C D E F G

HARCOURT SOCIAL Studies

This book provides the answers to the activities in the Homework and Practice Book, Student Edition. The table of contents below is organized into three columns. The first column lists the page numbers in this Teacher Edition. The second column identifies the Lesson, Skill, or Review activities shown on each page. The third column correlates the page content to pages in the Homework and Practice Book, Student Edition.

Contents

UNIT 1: THE LAND AND EARLY PEOPLE

Chapter 1: Our Nation's Geography

Page	Content	Student HP Book Pages
1	Lesson 1; Skill 1	pp. 1–2
2	Skill 1 (cont.); Lesson 2	pp. 3–4
3	Lesson 3; Lesson 4	pp. 5–6
4	Lesson 5	pp. 7–8
5	Skill 2; Study Guide	pp. 9–10
6	Study Guide (cont.); Summarize the Chapter	pp. 11–12

Chapter 2: Native Americans

Page	Content	Student HP Book Pages
7	Lesson 1; Skill 1	pp. 13–14
8	Skill 1 (cont.); Lesson 2	pp. 15–16
9	Lesson 3; Lesson 4	pp. 17–18
10	Lesson 5; Study Guide	pp. 19–20
11	Study Guide (cont.); Summarize the Chapter	pp. 21–22

UNIT 2: CULTURES MEET

Chapter 3: The Age of Exploration

Page	Content	Student HP Book Pages
12	Lesson 1; Lesson 2	pp. 23–24
13	Lesson 3: Skill 1	pp. 25–26
14	Skill 1 (cont.); Lesson 4	pp. 27–28
15	Study Guide	pp. 29–30
16	Summarize the Chapter	p. 31

Chapter 4: Building the First Colonies

Page	Content	Student HP Book Pages
16	Lesson 1	p. 32
17	Lesson 2	pp. 33–34
18	Skill 1	pp. 35–36
19	Lesson 3; Skill 2	pp. 37–38
20	Lesson 4; Study Guide	pp. 39–40
21	Study Guide (cont.); Summarize the Chapter	pp. 41–42

UNIT 3: THE THIRTEEN COLONIES

Chapter 5: The New England Colonies

Page	Content	Student HP Book Pages
22	Lesson 1	pp. 43–44
23	Skills 1; Lesson 2	pp. 45–46
24	Lesson 2 (cont.); Lesson 3	pp. 47–48
25	Study Guide	pp. 49–50
26	Summarize the Chapter	p. 51

Chapter 6: The Middle Colonies

Page	Content	Student HP Book Pages
26	Lesson 1	p. 52
27	Lesson 2	pp. 53–54
28	Lesson 3	pp. 55–56
29	Skill 1; Study Guide	pp. 57–58
30	Study Guide (cont.); Summarize the Chapter	pp. 59–60

Chapter 7: The Southern Colonies

Page	Content	Student HP Book Pages
31	Lesson 1	pp. 61–62
32	Skill 1	pp. 63–64
33	Lesson 2; Lesson 3	pp. 65–66
34	Study Guide	pp. 67–68
35	Summarize the Chapter	p. 69

UNIT 4: THE AMERICAN REVOLUTION

Chapter 8: The Colonies Unite

Page	Content	Student HP Book Pages
35	Lesson 1	p. 70
36	Skill 1	pp. 71–72
37	Lesson 2; Lesson 3	pp. 73–74
38	Lesson 4; Lesson 5	pp. 75–76
39	Skill 2; Study Guide	pp. 77–78
40	Study Guide (cont.); Summarize the Chapter	pp. 79–80

Chapter 9: The Revolutionary War

Page	Content	Student HP Book Pages
41	Lesson 1; Skill 1	pp. 81–82
42	Skill 1 (cont.); Lesson 2	pp. 83–84
43	Lesson 2 (cont.); Lesson 3	pp. 85–86
44	Skill 2; Lesson 4	pp. 87–88
45	Chapter Study Guide	pp. 89–90
46	Summarize the Chapter	p. 91

UNIT 5: A GROWING NATION

Chapter 10: The Constitution

Page	Content	Student HP Book Pages
46	Lesson 1	p. 92
47	Skill 1; Lesson 2	pp. 93–94
48	Lesson 3	pp. 95–96
49	Skill 2	pp. 97–98
50	Lesson 4; Study Guide	pp. 99–100
51	Study Guide (cont.); Summarize the Chapter	pp. 101–102

Chapter 11: The Young Republic

Page	Content	Student HP Book Pages
52	Lesson 1	pp. 103–104
53	Skill 1; Lesson 2	pp. 105–106
54	Lesson 3	pp. 107–108
55	Lesson 4; Study Guide	pp. 109–110
56	Study Guide (cont.); Summarize the Chapter	pp. 111–112

UNIT 6: CIVIL WAR TIMES

Chapter 12: The Civil War

Page	Content	Student HP Book Pages
57	Lesson 1	pp. 113–114
58	Lesson 2; Lesson 3	pp. 115–116
59	Lesson 3 (cont.); Lesson 4	pp. 117–118
60	Lesson 4 (cont.); Skill 1	pp. 119–120
61	Lesson 5; Study Guide	pp. 121–122
62	Study Guide (cont.); Summarize the Chapter	pp. 123–124

Chapter 13: A Changing Nation

Page	Content	Student HP Book Pages
63	Lesson 1; Lesson 2	pp. 125–126
64	Lesson 3	pp. 127–128
65	Skill 1	pp. 129–130
66	Lesson 4; Skill 2	pp. 131–132
67	Skill 2 (cont.); Study Guide	pp. 133–134
68	Study Guide (cont.); Summarize the Chapter	pp. 135–136

Name _____ Date _____

States and Regions

DIRECTIONS Use the map to answer the questions.

Regions of the United States

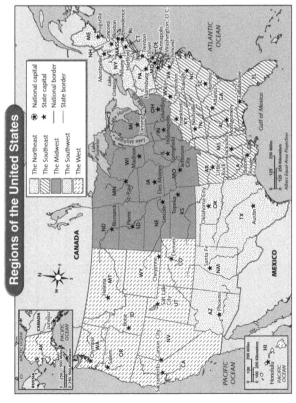

Legend:
- ⊛ National capital
- ★ State capital
- — National border
- — State border

- The Northeast
- The Southeast
- The Midwest
- The Southwest
- The West

1 The capitals of the states in the Southwest region are Phoenix, Santa Fe,

Oklahoma City, and __Austin__ .

2 The two states that are not contiguous with the rest of the United States are

Alaska and __Hawaii__ .

3 The region in the middle of the country is the __Midwest__ .

4 The smallest state in the Northeast region is __Rhode Island__ .

5 Florida is in the __Southeast__ region of the United States.

Use after reading Chapter 1, Lesson 1, pages 14–19.   **Homework and Practice Book ■ 1**

Name _____ Date _____

Skills: Use Latitude and Longitude

DIRECTIONS Use the map to find each latitude and longitude given below, and then write the name of the state in each location.

United States Latitude and Longitude

Legend:
- ⊛ National capital
- ★ State capital
- — National border
- — State border

1 30°N, 100°W   __Texas__

2 40°N, 90°W   __Illinois__

3 40°N, 80°W   __Pennsylvania__

4 40°N, 110°W   __Utah__

5 30°N, 90°W   __Louisiana__

Use after reading Chapter 1, Skill Lesson, pages 20–21.   (continued)

2 ■ Homework and Practice Book

© Harcourt

The Land

DIRECTIONS Fill in the missing information about landforms. Use the terms from the box to help you complete the sentences.

mountain range	basin	climate
mountains	Coastal	Interior

1. The kind of weather a place has over a long time is called its **climate**.

2. The **Coastal** Plain begins along the coast of Massachusetts as a strip of land no more than 10 miles wide.

3. The Appalachians are a **mountain range** that runs from southern Canada to central Alabama.

4. The **Interior** Plains stretch across the middle of the United States.

5. A **basin** is low, bowl-shaped land with higher land all around it.

6. Low **mountains** give the Pacific a rocky, rugged look.

Use after reading Chapter 1, Lesson 2, pages 22–29.

DIRECTIONS Describe the absolute location of each state capital. Use the map on page 2 to find the approximate latitude and longitude for each capital listed, and complete the chart below.

State Capital	Latitude	Longitude
Denver, Colorado	40°N	105°W
Trenton, New Jersey	40°N	75°W
Springfield, Illinois	40°N	90°W
Pierre, South Dakota	44°N	100°W
Tallahassee, Florida	30°N	85°W

DIRECTIONS Use the map on page 2 to find each state capital for the approximate latitude and longitude given, and complete the chart below.

Latitude	Longitude	State Capital
41°N	105°W	Cheyenne, Wyoming
43°N	85°W	Lansing, Michigan
39°N	120°W	Carson City, Nevada
30°N	98°W	Austin, Texas
45°N	93°W	St. Paul, Minnesota

Use after reading Chapter 1, Skill Lesson, pages 20–21.

Climate and Vegetation

DIRECTIONS Use the map to answer the questions below.

Climate Regions of the United States

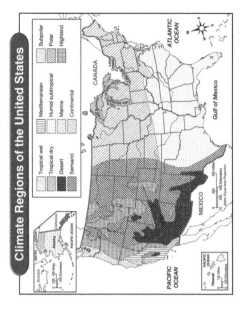

Legend:
- Tropical wet
- Tropical dry
- Desert
- Semiarid
- Mediterranean
- Humid subtropical
- Marine
- Continental
- Subpolar
- Polar
- Highland

1. Which two climate regions does Alaska have? __subpolar and polar__

2. Which part of the United States has a mostly desert and semiarid climate? __the southwest__

3. The climate found in the southeastern part of the United States is mostly __humid subtropical__ .

4. A Mediterranean climate occurs in parts of __California__ .

5. The climate in most of the Midwest region of the United States is similar to that of the __Northeast__ region.

Use after reading Chapter 1, Lesson 4, pages 36–39.

Bodies of Water

DIRECTIONS Use the map to answer the questions below.

Major Bodies of Water in the United States

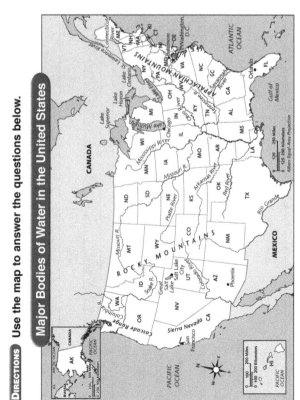

1. Name the five Great Lakes. __Superior, Michigan, Huron, Erie, and Ontario__

2. Name five states that border the Gulf of Mexico. __Texas, Louisiana, Mississippi, Alabama, Florida__

3. Name three tributaries of the Mississippi River. Possible responses: __the Missouri, Ohio, Arkansas, and Red Rivers__

4. Name the four states through which the Arkansas River flows. __Arkansas, Oklahoma, Kansas, and Colorado__

Use after reading Chapter 1, Lesson 3, pages 30–34.

Name _____ Date _____

People and the Environment

DIRECTIONS Choose the word from the box that best answers the question. Then write it in the space provided.

efficiency	modify	nonrenewable
renewable	transportation	

1 People often need to live near **transportation** routes.

2 A resource that can be made again by people or by nature is **renewable**.

3 A **nonrenewable** resource cannot be made again by nature or by people.

4 People **modify** the land to live in difficult areas and meet their needs.

5 Many of the cars people drive today have better **efficiency** than cars made years ago.

DIRECTIONS Write the name of the resource in the correct column. Then list another renewable resource and another nonrenewable resource.

wind	coal	trees
		oil

Renewable Resources	Nonrenewable Resources
wind	coal
trees	oil
Students list a renewable resource.	Students list a nonrenewable resource.

(continued)

© Harcourt

Name _____ Date _____

DIRECTIONS Choose the best term from the box to complete the sentences.

Coastal Plain	fresh water	mountains
natural resources	irrigation	

1 Many colonists settled where there was farmland and **fresh water**.

2 At first, most people avoided settling in the desert, tundra, and **mountains**.

3 Most farming in the United States takes place on the **Coastal Plain**, on the Interior Plains, and in valleys in the West.

4 Two examples of **natural resources** are soil and plants.

5 **Irrigation** allows farmers to grow crops in areas that do not receive much rainfall.

© Harcourt

Skills: Read Time Lines

DIRECTIONS Read the time line below. Then answer the questions.

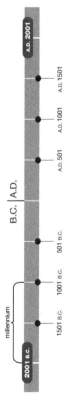

1 What do some people today mean when they refer to the term B.C.?
Some people use B.C. to refer to the time before Christ
was born.

2 What do some people today mean when they refer to the term A.D.?
Some people use A.D. to refer to the time after Christ
was born.

3 How many millennia are shown on the time line? ___ 4

4 How many centuries are shown on the time line? ___ 40

5 Which year came earlier, 1500 B.C. or 600 B.C.?
1500 B.C. came earlier

6 Which year came later, 700 B.C. or 900 A.D.? ___ 900 A.D.

Chapter 1

Chapter Study Guide

DIRECTIONS Fill in the missing information in these paragraphs about the geography of the United States. Use the terms listed below to help you complete the paragraphs.

Lesson 1	Lesson 2	Lesson 3	Lesson 4	Lesson 5
contiguous	Sierra Nevada	Great Lakes	orbit	mining
location	Appalachian	inlets	equator	farming
Canada	Coastal Plain	Great Salt Lake	vegetation	efficiency
regions	Rocky	tributaries	elevation	physical

Lesson 1 The United States is a nation made of up 50 states. Forty-eight of them are _____ **contiguous** _____, or next to each other. Hawaii and Alaska are separated from the other states. The 50 states are grouped into five large _____ **regions** _____. These are the West, the Southwest, the Midwest, the Southeast, and the Northeast. Each region is based on its relative _____ **location** _____ in the United States. To the north of the United States is _____ **Canada** _____. The United States' southern neighbor is Mexico.

Lesson 2 The United States is a land of many different kinds of places. The _____ **Coastal Plain** _____ stretches along the Atlantic Ocean from Massachusetts to Florida. It extends west into Texas and Mexico. The tree-covered _____ **Appalachian** _____ Mountains are the oldest mountains in the United States. Farther west is the nation's largest and longest mountain range, the _____ **Rocky** _____ Mountains. The _____ **Sierra Nevada** _____ lies just inside California.

(continued)

Homework and Practice Book Teacher Edition ■ 5

Name _____ Date _____

Summarize the Chapter

COMPARE AND CONTRAST

DIRECTIONS Complete the graphic organizers below to compare and contrast two geographic regions of the United States.

Topic 1
Name of Region

Topic 2
Name of Region

Similar
Students will list similarities in chosen regions.

Topic 1
Name of Region

Topic 2
Name of Region

Different
Students will list differences in chosen regions.

© Harcourt

Name _____ Date _____

Lesson 3 The shape of the United States is in part defined by the
___inlets___ along the Atlantic and Pacific Coasts.

These areas of water extend into the land from larger bodies of water. The
largest lakes in North America are the ___Great Lakes___ .

Another large lake is the ___Great Salt Lake___ , which is as
salty as any ocean. Rivers and their ___tributaries___ make
up river systems.

Lesson 4 The climate of a place depends partly on its distance from the
___equator___ . Places close to it tend to be warmer
than places that are farther away. ___Elevation___
and water also affect climate. Changes in seasons are caused by Earth's
___orbit___ . The ___vegetation___
in the United States varies according to temperature and precipitation.

Lesson 5 Today, almost 300 million people live in the United States.
___Physical___ features, such as climate, water, and
landforms, can affect where people settle. About half of the land in the
United States is used for ___farming___ . Much of the
___mining___ takes place in mountain regions.

Americans use tools to modify the land to gather and use natural
resources. Still, people today understand that they need to use
___efficiency___ when using them so that they do not
run out.

© Harcourt

Name _____ Date _____

Skills: Use a Cultural Map

DIRECTIONS Use the map to answer the questions on page 15.

Early Cultures of the Southwest

UNITED STATES

MEXICO

ATLANTIC OCEAN

Gulf of Mexico

PACIFIC OCEAN

Rio Grande

Colorado River

HUALAPAI
HAVASUPAI
MOJAVE
YAVAPAI
YUMA
TOHONO O'ODHAM
PIMA
PIMA
YAQUI
HUICHOL
COAHUILTEC
APACHE
APACHE
PUEBLO
ZUNI
HOPI
NAVAJO
APACHE

HOPI Settlement area of Native Americans
Present-day border
Southwest Cultural Region

0 150 300 Miles
0 150 300 Kilometers
Albers Equal-Area Projection

(continued)

Use after reading Chapter 2, Skill Lesson, pages 60–61.

© Harcourt

Name _____ Date _____

Early People

DIRECTIONS Fill in the blanks in the sentences below, using terms from the box.

class	ancestors	civilization	migration	theory

1 The first people in North America many thousands of years ago are **ancestors**, or early family members, of present-day Native Americans.

2 A **theory** is an idea based on study and research.

3 Many scientists believe that about 12,000 years ago, groups of hunters and their families took part in a **migration** across the land bridge from Asia to North America.

4 A **civilization** is a group of people with ways of life, religion, and learning.

5 At the top of the Mayan **class** structure were the religious leaders.

Use after reading Chapter 2, Lesson 1, pages 52–59.

© Harcourt

Name _____ Date _____

The Eastern Woodlands

DIRECTIONS Read the passage. Then answer the questions that follow.

In the late 1500s, Iroquois tribes fought among themselves. Often these battles were over control of hunting areas. According to one story, an Iroquois named Deganawida convinced a Mohawk leader named Hiawatha to join him in spreading the message that "All shall receive the Great Law and labor together for the welfare of man."

The result was a confederation called the Iroquois League. The league was made up of the Five Nations of the Seneca, the Cayuga, the Onondaga, the Oneida, and the Mohawk. A few years later, a sixth nation, the Tuscarora, joined the league.

Each nation in the league governed itself, and problems were often solved by a vote. Important matters that affected all the league's nations, such as war, were made by a Grand Council of 50 chiefs from all nations.

① Who was Deganawida?

a man who wanted the Iroquois to stop fighting

② Why did Deganawida think it was important to stop the fighting?

to protect the Iroquois way of life

③ Which tribes belonged to the Iroquois League?

the Seneca, Cayuga, Onondaga, Oneida, Mohawk, and Tuscarora

④ Which group made decisions that affected all the league's nations?

a Grand Council of 50 chiefs

⑤ What do you think Deganawida meant when he said, "All shall receive the Great Law and labor together for the welfare of man"?

The tribes should work together for their own good.

Use after reading Chapter 2, Lesson 2, pages 62–67.

© Harcourt

Name _____ Date _____

① Which people lived in present-day Mexico?

Tohono O'Odham, Pima, Yaqui, Coahuiltec, Huichol

② Which people lived closest to the Colorado River? Havasupai, Hualapai, Mojave, Yuma, and Tohono O'Odham

③ Which people lived along a coast?

Tohono O'Odham, Yaqui, Coahuiltec, Huichol

④ Which people lived the farthest east?

Coahuiltec

⑤ Which people lived the farthest south?

Huichol

⑥ What river flows through Apache lands?

Rio Grande

⑦ Which people had the most widespread settlements?

Apache

⑧ Why do you think the Navajo learned certain customs from the Hopi rather than from the Pima?

Hopi tribes lived closer to the Navajo than to the Pima.

⑨ Which people lived closest to the mouth of the Colorado River?

Tohono O'Odham

⑩ Which people lived in parts of present-day Mexico and in the United States?

Pima

Use after reading Chapter 2, Skill Lesson, pages 60–61.

© Harcourt

The Southwest and the West

DIRECTIONS Fill in the blanks in the sentences below, using terms from the box.

adapt	buffalo	trade networks	staple	surplus

1 Native Americans had to ____adapt____ their ways of life to the land.

2 Corn, beans, and squash were the ____staple____ foods of the Pueblo people.

3 Pueblo people found ways to collect water and to store ____surplus____ food.

4 The Shoshone spent part of the year in the mountains hunting ____buffalo____.

5 Some Native Americans formed ____trade networks____ to get goods they could not make or find themselves.

Use after reading Chapter 2, Lesson 4, pages 76–80.

(continued)

The Plains

DIRECTIONS Read the labels above the boxes. Draw a picture of each item.

Lodge	Tepee
Drawings will vary but should resemble a round house.	Drawings will vary but should resemble a cone-shaped tent.

Travois	Sod
Drawings will vary but should resemble a carrier.	Drawings will vary but should resemble grass.

DIRECTIONS Choose one of the items you drew. Write a sentence or two describing how the item was made or used.

Answers will vary. Possible response: Some Plains people lived in tepees. Tepees were easy to build and move.

Use after reading Chapter 2, Lesson 3, pages 70–75.

Name _____ Date _____

The Northwest and the Arctic

DIRECTIONS Read each question below, and choose the best answer. Then fill in the circle for the answer you have chosen.

1 Which objects did the Northwest Coast people NOT make from wood?

- (A) dishes
- (B) spoons
- (C) pottery
- (D) utensils

2 Which is NOT true about totem poles?

- (A) They were made of wood.
- (B) They showed characters used to tell stories.
- (C) They welcomed visitors.
- (D) They were made only by women.

3 How did the Inuit and the Aleut get much of their food?

- (A) by hunting
- (B) by farming
- (C) by trading
- (D) by gathering

4 What did the Inuit and the Aleut use to make most of their tools?

- (A) iron
- (B) bones
- (C) wood
- (D) stones

5 What did the Inuit use to build igloos?

- (A) stones
- (B) wood
- (C) adobe
- (D) ice

Use after reading Chapter 2, Lesson 5, pages 82–87.

© Harcourt

Chapter **2**

Name _____ Date _____

Study Guide

DIRECTIONS Fill in the missing information in these paragraphs about Native Americans. Use the terms listed below to help you complete the paragraph for each lesson.

Lesson 1	Lesson 2	Lesson 3	Lesson 4	Lesson 5
hunted	confederation	council	trade networks	bartered
theory	Iroquois	tepees	staple	clan
ancestors	Algonquian	sod	surplus	igloos

Lesson 1 The first people in North America are the __ancestors__ of present-day Native Americans. According to one __theory__, those people crossed Beringia from Asia to reach North America. Another theory says that early people may have traveled to the Americas by boat. When they got there, many people __hunted__ giant animals. In about 3,000 B.C., Native Americans began planting seeds and growing crops.

Lesson 2 The __Iroquois__ lived near the Great Lakes, in what is now Pennsylvania, New York, and the Lake Ontario region of Canada. They farmed and lived in villages. In the 1500s, they formed a __confederation__ to settle their disputes. The __Algonquian__ lived on the Coastal Plain. Because of the plentiful supply of fish near the coast, the tribes relied less on growing crops.

(continued)

Use after reading Chapter 2, pages 52–91.

© Harcourt

Name _____ Date _____

Summarize the Chapter

⭐ Focus Skill **COMPARE AND CONTRAST**

DIRECTIONS Complete the graphic organizers to compare and contrast the Native American groups who lived in different regions of North America.

Topic 1

Some groups relied more on hunting for food.

Similar

They adapted their way of life to their environment.

_____
_____
_____
_____

Topic 2

Some groups relied more on farming for food.

Topic 1

Iroquois

used trees to make canoes and shelters; hunted and gathered in northeastern parts; farmed in southern parts

Similar

Both groups hunted and gathered; both farmed; both used resources to make tools.

Topic 2

Algonquian

relied more on fish than the Iroquois; used animal bones and wood to make hooks and fishing traps

---

Name _____ Date _____

Lesson 3 Plains people all hunted buffalo, but they had varied ways of life. Some people built lodges covered with ___**sod**___. Other groups used buffalo skins to make tents called ___**tepees**___. Among the Lakota, each group made its own choices. The Cheyenne leaders gathered as a ___**council**___ to make decisions that all Cheyenne followed. Buffalo were the main source of food for all the Native American groups that lived on the Great Plains.

Lesson 4 The people of the Southwest and the West had to adapt to their environment. The Southwest people grew their ___**staple**___ foods, such as corn, beans, and squash. Because their land was so dry, they had to collect water and store ___**surplus**___ food. People of the West depended on rivers and oceans for food. Other Native Americans formed ___**trade networks**___ to meet their needs.

Lesson 5 In the Northwest, the members of a ___**clan**___ lived in the same longhouse. To meet their needs, the clans ___**bartered**___ for goods at trading centers, such as The Dalles. In the Arctic, people lived in ___**igloos**___ made of ice. They hunted whales and seals for food and clothing. Since resources were limited, Arctic people made everything out of what they hunted, including tools.

A Changing World

DIRECTIONS Read each statement about the goals, troubles, and triumphs of the explorers listed below. In the space provided, write the name of the explorer who would have been most likely to have made the statement.

Balboa	Cabot	Magellan	Vespucci

1. "I sailed to a place south of where Columbus had landed, but the places I saw did not match Polo's descriptions of Asia." **Vespucci**

2. "I led the first European expedition to reach the Pacific Ocean." **Balboa**

3. "It took us more than three months to cross the Pacific Ocean, and many of my crew died of hunger and illness." **Magellan**

4. "The English king sent me on an expedition to the Indies to help England compete for land and wealth." **Cabot**

5. "My goal is to lead the first expedition to sail around the world." **Magellan**

6. "A German mapmaker named a continent after me." **Vespucci**

7. "I helped settlers start a settlement in what is now the country of Panama." **Balboa**

8. "I led the first expedition to reach Asia by sailing west across the Pacific Ocean." **Magellan**

9. "When I reached what I thought was China, I saw what my son would one day describe as 'a very sterile [lonely] land.'" **Cabot**

10. "I figured out that Earth is larger than most people thought." **Vespucci**

Use after reading Chapter 3, Lesson 2, pages 120–125.

Exploration and Technology

DIRECTIONS Fill in the missing words in this letter from Christopher Columbus to Queen Isabella. Use the terms from the box.

technology
expedition
benefits
empire
costs

Dear Queen Isabella,

Thank you for agreeing to pay for my   **expedition** . With a better compass and astrolabe, I am sure that I have the   **technology**   I need to reach Asia. As you know, the   **costs**   of the trip are high. But I promise you that the   **benefits**   also will be high. Your   **empire**   will gain great wealth and vast lands.

Your servant,

Christopher Columbus

Use after reading Chapter 3, Lesson 1, pages 110–117.

Name _____ Date _____

Skills: Use an Elevation Map

DIRECTIONS Add details to the map as described in each item below.

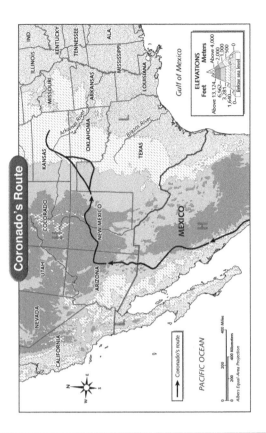

Coronado's Route

→ Coronado's route

PACIFIC OCEAN

ELEVATIONS
Feet   Meters
Above 13,124   Above 4,000
6,562   2,000
3,281   1,000
1,640   500
0   0
Below sea level

IND. • ILLINOIS • MISSOURI • KENTUCKY • TENNESSEE • ARKANSAS • ALA. • MISSISSIPPI • LOUISIANA • OKLAHOMA • KANSAS • COLORADO • UTAH • NEVADA • CALIFORNIA • ARIZONA • NEW MEXICO • TEXAS • MEXICO

Arkansas River • Brazos River • Gulf of Mexico

Albers Equal-Area Projection
0   200   400 Miles
0   200   400 Kilometers

① Write an *H* on any part of the map that shows the highest elevation in the region.
See map for examples of correct placement.

② Write an *L* on any part of the map that shows the lowest elevation in the region.
See map for examples of correct placement.

(continued)

26 ▪ Homework and Practice Book   Use after reading Chapter 3, Skill Lesson, pages 136–137.

© Harcourt

Name _____ Date _____

Spanish Explorations

DIRECTIONS Study the map. Then answer the questions about the routes of Spanish explorers and the distances they traveled.

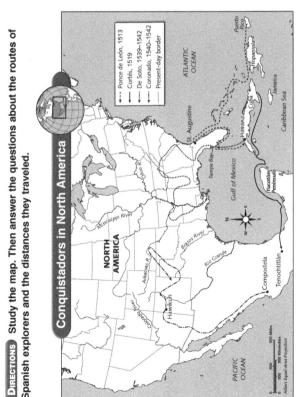

Conquistadors in North America

NORTH AMERICA

PACIFIC OCEAN

ATLANTIC OCEAN

Ponce de León, 1513
Cortés, 1519
De Soto, 1539–1542
Coronado, 1540–1542
Present-day border

St. Augustine • Tampa Bay • Havana • Cuba • Jamaica • Hispaniola • Puerto Rico • Caribbean Sea • Gulf of Mexico • Yucatán Peninsula • Tenochtitlán • Compostela • Hawikuh • Mississippi River • Ohio R. • Arkansas R. • Brazos River • Rio Grande • Colorado R.

Albers Equal-Area Projection
0   500   Miles
0   500   Kilometers

① Which conquistador traveled the longest distance on land? **Coronado**

② Which conquistador crossed the Mississippi River? **De Soto**

③ Which conquistadors reached the Arkansas River? **De Soto and Coronado**

④ Which conquistador traveled the farthest north? **Coronado**

⑤ Which conquistadors traveled through present-day Mexico?
Cortés and Coronado

⑥ Which conquistador started his exploration in Puerto Rico?
Ponce de León

Use after reading Chapter 3, Lesson 3, pages 128–134.   Homework and Practice Book ▪ 25

© Harcourt

Other Nations Explore

DIRECTIONS Imagine that you are Giovanni da Verrazano and that you are being interviewed by a newspaper reporter. Write answers to the interview questions.

1 Mr. Verrazano, what was the goal of your voyages to the west?
Possible response: I wanted to find the
Northwest Passage to gain
wealth and power for France.

2 Who sent you to find the Northwest Passage?
Possible response: The French king,
Francis I, sent me to find the Northwest
Passage through North America.

3 What was the biggest problem that you faced?
Possible response: I found a long coastline, but I could not
find a water route to Asia.

4 You did not achieve your goal, but what did you do?
Possible response: I explored miles of coastline unknown before
to Europeans. I also met some of the people who live there.

5 What were these people like?
Possible response: They were friendly.

DIRECTIONS Use the map on page 26 to answer these questions.

3 What is the range of elevation in feet along the Brazos River?
0, or sea level, to 3,281 feet

4 What is the highest range of elevation in feet along Coronado's route?
6,562 to 13,124 feet

5 What was the range of elevation in feet on the route through Mexico?
0, or sea level, to 13,124 feet

6 How would land elevation have changed if Coronado had traveled 150 miles due west from what is today Arizona instead of east toward New Mexico?
The land elevation would have become lower.

7 How would you describe the land elevation at the start of his journey in North America?
First, the land elevation is low. Then the land rises.

8 How would you describe the land elevation toward the end of his journey?
The land elevation lowers through the mountains.

9 What kind of landform would you expect to find at the highest elevations to the north of Coronado's route?
Possible response: mountains

10 Write a sentence describing the land that the Arkansas River flows through.
Possible response: The river moves down through the mountains
into low land.

Name _____ Date _____

Lesson 2 Other explorers followed Columbus across the Atlantic. John Cabot sailed west to present-day **Newfoundland**. Cabot thought that he had reached Asia. **Amerigo Vespucci** knew that Cabot was wrong, though. He realized that Cabot and other explorers had found a continent that Europeans did not know about. Vasco Núñez de Balboa found the key to reaching Asia. He crossed an **isthmus** and saw the Pacific Ocean. The sailors on **Ferdinand Magellan** 's ship were the first Europeans to travel around the world.

Lesson 3 The ruler of Spain encouraged explorers to find riches in lands that Spain had claimed. Spain offered **grants** to those who led expeditions. These men were known as **conquistadors** .

The Catholic Church also wanted to spread its power to the Americas. For that reason, it sent **missionaries** to convert Native Americans to the Catholic Church.

Lesson 4 Other explorers still hoped to find another route to Asia. This route became known as the **Northwest Passage** . Jacques Cartier traveled up the **St. Lawrence River** , hoping that it would lead to Asia. Henry Hudson explored other rivers and bays with the same goal. Hudson failed, and his crew led a **mutiny** and set him adrift.

Use after reading Chapter 3, pages 110–145.

Chapter 3

Name _____ Date _____

Study Guide

DIRECTIONS Fill in the missing information in these paragraphs about European exploration of the Americas. Use the terms and names below to help you complete the paragraphs for each lesson.

Lesson 1	Lesson 2	Lesson 3	Lesson 4
technology	isthmus	missionaries	St. Lawrence River
benefits	Ferdinand Magellan	grants	mutiny
navigation	Amerigo Vespucci	conquistadors	Northwest Passage
expedition	Newfoundland		
entrepreneur			

Lesson 1 In the 1400s, Europeans entered into a new age of learning, science, and art called the Renaissance. They read about the riches of Asia, but they did not have the knowledge and the tools to reach Asia by sea. To help solve these problems, Prince Henry of Portugal started a school to teach **navigation** . People at the school created new kinds of **technology** , including better compasses and astrolabes.

Christopher Columbus led an **expedition** with the goal of sailing west to Asia. Like other explorers, Columbus was an **entrepreneur** . He convinced Queen Isabella to pay for his trip by promising her **benefits** , such as riches from Asia.

(continued)

Use after reading Chapter 3, pages 110–145.

Homework and Practice Book Teacher Edition ■ 15

The Spanish Colonies

DIRECTIONS Read the paragraphs. Then answer the questions below.

Santa Fe, New Mexico

In 1598, Juan de Oñate led a large group of people from Mexico north to what would become the Spanish colony of New Mexico. That same year, Oñate built the headquarters of the colony at the San Juan pueblo. This settlement extended the Camino Real by about 600 miles.

In about 1610, Pedro de Peralta led the settlers in building a city high on a plateau, where the climate was cooler than it was in the desert. They named the city Santa Fe. The name is Spanish for "holy faith." It was the first permanent European settlement in western North America. New settlers and missionaries later arrived in the city. Santa Fe became the capital of Spain's territory in New Mexico.

1. Who led the first group of people to New Mexico? **Juan de Oñate**

2. Which city was the capital of New Mexico? **Santa Fe**

3. By how much did Juan de Oñate extend the Camino Real? **about 600 miles**

4. Why did the settlers build their city on a plateau? **because the climate was cooler than in the desert**

5. When was the first permanent European settlement in western North America built? **in about 1610**

32 ■ Homework and Practice Book

Use after reading Chapter 4, Lesson 1, pages 148–152.

© Harcourt

Summarize the Chapter

★ MAIN IDEA AND DETAILS

DIRECTIONS Complete this graphic organizer to show that you understand the main idea and supporting details about European explorations of the Americas.

Main Idea

Europeans explored and claimed lands in the Americas.

Details

Possible response: Columbus sailed west and reached land across the Atlantic Ocean.	Possible response: After Columbus's voyages, rulers sent explorers across the Atlantic Ocean to claim new lands.	Possible response: Spanish conquistadors looked for gold and claimed land in the Americas for Spain.	Possible response: Explorers sent by France and England explored the east coast of North America in search of both riches and the Northwest Passage.

Use after reading Chapter 3, pages 110–145.

Homework and Practice Book ■ 31

© Harcourt

---

16 ■ **Homework and Practice Book Teacher Edition**

Name _____ Date _____

The Virginia Colony

DIRECTIONS Complete the organizer to show important facts about the settlers who founded Jamestown.

The Founding of Jamestown

Who	What	When	Where	Why
A group of 105 colonists arrived in Virginia.	They planted crops and built a fort.	1607	They built on swampy land along the James River.	They hoped to get rich and find gold.

DIRECTIONS Using the lines provided, write one fact that tells how each person was important to the survival of the Jamestown settlers.

King James I
He let a group of colonists try to start another colony in Virginia. That colony became Jamestown.

John Smith
He made a rule that said that colonists who did not work did not eat. Soon colonists were planting crops and building a fort.

Pocahontas
Pocahontas helped bring about a short time of peace at Jamestown.

(continued)

Name _____ Date _____

DIRECTIONS Use your completed organizer to help you write a narrative about life in early Jamestown. Your narrative may include facts that are not on the organizer.

John Smith

Pocahontas

Possible response:

In 1607, a group of 105 colonists settled along the James River. They named the settlement Jamestown in honor of the English king, James I. They built it on swampy land. The colonists had come to Virginia hoping to get rich, but many of them did not want to work hard. When John Smith took over as their leader, he made a rule that anyone who did not work did not eat. The colonists began planting crops and building a fort.

Page 35

Name _____ Date _____

Skills: Compare Primary and Secondary Sources

DIRECTIONS Study the photo and illustration below. Use the information they contain to answer questions about primary and secondary sources.

1. Is the title page of the book shown a primary or a secondary source? How can you tell?
   Primary. The year 1612 is written on the title page of the book. This tells when the book was published.

2. How can you tell that the picture of the Virginia settler is a secondary source?
   The picture is a photograph of a historical reenactor.

3. What do the two sources have in common?
   They both show information about life in the Virginia Colony.

(continued)

Page 36

Name _____ Date _____

DIRECTIONS This modern drawing shows what the houses built outside the Jamestown fort may have looked like in the early 1600s. Use it to answer the questions that follow.

4. Why did Jamestown settlers have fields so close to their homes?
   Possible response: They were afraid of being attacked.

5. Is the drawing of Jamestown a primary or a secondary source? Explain why.
   Possible response: The drawing is a secondary source because it is a modern drawing. The person who made it did not live during the time when Jamestown was founded.

Skills: Solve a Problem

DIRECTIONS Imagine that, after a long journey on the *Mayflower*, you have finally reached land. When you arrive on shore, you realize that you are not in Virginia. You wonder how the Pilgrims will get along with no government. Use the steps below to help you solve the problem.

Step 1: Identify the problem.

There is no government to make laws or keep order.

Step 2: Gather information.

Possible response: The men meet to decide what law they should follow.

Step 3: List possible solutions.

We can continue to follow Dutch ways, or we can found our own government.

Step 4: Consider the advantages and disadvantages of each solution.

Possible response: We left Holland so that we would not have to follow Dutch ways. On the other hand, setting up a new government is hard.

Step 5: Choose the best solution.

Possible response: We will set up our own form of government.

Step 6: Try your solution.

Imagine yourself applying the solution you chose. Think through what might happen and what the results might be.

Step 7: Tell about how well your solution helped solve the problem.

Possible response: The men wrote the Mayflower Compact, introducing majority rule and giving the signers a voice in government.

Use after reading Chapter 4, Skill Lesson, pages 168–169.

© Harcourt

The Plymouth Colony

DIRECTIONS When the Mayflower Compact was written in 1620, the English language was very different from what it is today. Below is a version of the Mayflower Compact written in present-day language. Use it to answer the questions that follow.

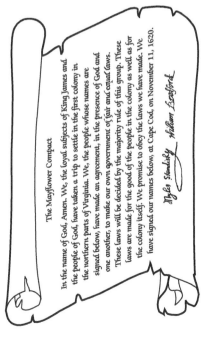

The Mayflower Compact

In the name of God, Amen. We, the loyal subjects of King James and the people of God, have taken a trip to settle in the first colony in the northern parts of Virginia. We, the people whose names are signed below, have made an agreement, in the presence of God and one another, to make our own government of fair and equal laws. These laws will be decided by the majority rule of this group. These laws are made for the good of the people in the colony as well as for the colony itself. We promise to obey the laws we have made. We have signed our names below, at Cape Cod, on November 11, 1620.

Myles Standing   William Bradford

1 Who is the English ruler named in the Mayflower Compact?
   King James I

2 Where did the Mayflower passengers think they were going to settle?
   in the northern parts of Virginia

3 How did the writers of the Mayflower Compact say laws would be decided?
   by majority rule

4 What did the passengers promise?
   They promised to obey the laws they made.

5 Where and when was the Mayflower Compact signed?
   It was signed at Cape Cod on November 11, 1620.

Use after reading Chapter 4, Lesson 3, pages 162–167.

© Harcourt

Name _____ Date _____

The French and the Dutch

DIRECTIONS Read each question below, and choose the best answer. Then fill in the circle for the answer you have chosen.

1 Why did French merchants help set up settlements in North America?

- Ⓐ They wanted the Native Americans' gold.
- Ⓑ They wanted wealth that came from the fur trade.
- Ⓒ They wanted to control the route to Asia.
- Ⓓ They wanted to force the Spanish off their land.

2 What was the aim of Dutch settlers coming to North America?

- Ⓐ to profit from the fur trade
- Ⓑ to find good farmland
- Ⓒ to escape war in Europe
- Ⓓ to practice their religion

3 What kept Marquette and Joliet from reaching the mouth of the Mississippi River?

- Ⓐ They got lost.
- Ⓑ They ran out of food.
- Ⓒ They were attacked by Native Americans.
- Ⓓ They feared meeting Spanish soldiers.

4 Who was the first French explorer to reach the mouth of the Mississippi River?

- Ⓐ Jacques Cartier
- Ⓑ Samuel de Champlain
- Ⓒ Sieur de La Salle
- Ⓓ Pierre Le Moyne

5 What was one problem that early French settlements faced?

- Ⓐ The region of Louisiana failed to attract many people.
- Ⓑ Native Americans refused to trade with the French.
- Ⓒ Spanish soldiers attacked French forts.
- Ⓓ Colonies grew quickly, and good land was scarce.

Name _____ Date _____

Chapter **4**

Study Guide

DIRECTIONS Fill in the missing information in these paragraphs about the first colonies. Use the terms and names below to help you complete the paragraphs for each lesson.

Lesson 1	Lesson 2	Lesson 3	Lesson 4
haciendas	raw materials	Samoset	New Orleans
plantations	cash crop	Tisquantum	Quebec
missions	royal colony	William Bradford	New Amsterdam
borderlands	legislature		

Lesson 1   Some early Spanish settlers hoped to find gold. Others

started large farms. However, there were not enough workers to do all the

labor on a large farm. To find the workers they needed, some Spanish settlers

enslaved Native Americans to work on these **plantations** .

Spanish soldiers built forts to protect lands on the edge of New Spain.

Ranchers built large estates, or **haciendas** , in the outlying

lands. Spain did not want to lose these **borderlands** to other

countries. The Spanish also built **missions** , where Spanish

priests hoped to convert Native Americans to the Catholic religion.

(continued)

Summarize the Chapter

MAIN IDEA AND DETAILS

DIRECTIONS Complete this graphic organizer to show that you understand the main idea and some supporting details about the first European colonies in the Americas.

Main Idea

Europeans started colonies in North America.

Details

Possible response: The Spanish built plantations, forts, and missions throughout New Spain to keep control of lands they claimed.

Possible response: English colonists built settlements in Virginia, hoping to get rich.

Possible response: Another group of English colonists, the Pilgrims, settled in New England. They wanted to worship in their own way, and find economic opportunities.

Possible response: The Dutch and French started settlements to make money from the fur trade.

Use after reading Chapter 4, pages 148–179.

Lesson 2 England hoped to benefit from __raw materials__, such as lumber, from its Virginia Colony. The colonists were soon growing tobacco as a __cash crop__ to sell to Europe. As the colony grew, it needed laws to keep order. The Virginia __legislature__ was the first representative assembly in the English colonies. The Powhatan Wars led King James I to make Virginia a __royal colony__ in 1624.

Lesson 3 The Pilgrims settled in Massachusetts, where they had religious freedom. Among their leaders was __William Bradford__. The Native Americans that the Pilgrims met were helpful to them. An Abenaki named __Samoset__ welcomed the Pilgrims. He brought a Wampanoag named __Tisquantum__, who showed the settlers where to fish and how to plant food. Plymouth grew for some time until more people who were unfriendly to the Native Americans arrived.

Lesson 4 Samuel de Champlain founded __Quebec__. It was the first French settlement in North America. French settlements grew slowly. More than 100 years passed before the town of __New Orleans__ was founded. It became the capital of France's southern colony, Louisiana.

The Dutch competed with the French for the fur trade. The first Dutch colony was New Netherland, and its main trading center was __New Amsterdam__.

Use after reading Chapter 4, pages 148–179.

Name _____ Date _____

Settling New England

DIRECTIONS Read each statement below. Read the words in the box, and write the correct name on the blank provided. You may use some names more than once.

| Thomas Hooker | Anne Hutchinson | Metacomet |
| David Thomson | Roger Williams | John Winthrop |

1. This person lived with the Narragansett after being expelled from the Massachusetts Bay Colony. **Roger Williams**

2. This person founded a fishing settlement that became part of the New Hampshire Colony. **David Thomson**

3. This person was a leader of the group that settled Boston. **John Winthrop**

4. This person was a Puritan minister who disagreed with the way the leaders of Massachusetts ruled. **Thomas Hooker**

5. This person was expelled from the Massachusetts Bay Colony after being tried on charges of sedition. **Anne Hutchinson**

6. This person founded the Connecticut Colony. **Thomas Hooker**

7. This person decided that the Native Americans had to unite against the colonists. **Metacomet**

8. This person wanted his settlement to be seen as an example of Christian living. **John Winthrop**

9. This person founded a settlement that later joined with Providence and became part of Rhode Island. **Anne Hutchinson**

10. This person was elected governor of the Massachusetts Bay Colony. **John Winthrop**

(continued)

© Harcourt

Name _____ Date _____

DIRECTIONS Fill in the blanks to complete the web about settling New England.

More New England Settlements

Settling Boston

1. Leader: **John Winthrop**

2. Reason for founding: **to set up an example of Christian living**

3. Became part of which colony: **Massachusetts Bay**

Settling Providence

4. Leader: **Roger Williams**

5. Reason for founding: **expelled for spreading "new and dangerous opinions"**

6. Became part of which colony: **Rhode Island**

Settling Hartford

7. Leader: **Thomas Hooker**

8. Reason for founding: **disagreed with Massachusetts Bay Colony leaders**

9. Became part of which colony: **Connecticut**

Settling Portsmouth

10. Leader: **David Thomson**

11. Reason for founding: **looked for new economic opportunities**

12. Became part of which colony: **New Hampshire**

© Harcourt

Name _____ Date _____

Skills: Tell Fact from Opinion

DIRECTIONS Read each statement below. In the space provided, write **F** if the statement is a fact. Write **O** if the statement is an opinion.

1. **O** Boston was a perfect example of Christian living.

2. **F** John Winthrop's group of Puritans chose to build their "city upon a hill" to the south of Salem, near the mouth of the Charles River.

3. **F** In 1635, the leaders of Massachusetts voted to expel Roger Williams for dissent.

4. **O** I think the leaders were right in expelling Anne Hutchinson.

5. **F** In 1675, angry feelings between the colonists and the Native Americans led to war.

6. **O** The frontier was the best place to live.

DIRECTIONS Write one fact and one opinion about each person named below.

John Winthrop

7. Fact: **Possible response: He led the second group of Puritans to settle the Massachusetts Bay Colony.**

8. Opinion: **Possible response: He should not have tried to have such strict control of the Puritans.**

Roger Williams

9. Fact: **Possible response: He believed that the church should be separate from the colonial government.**

10. Opinion: **Possible response: I do not think that the ideas that Williams was spreading were "new and dangerous" opinions like the leaders said.**

Use after reading Chapter 5, Skill Lesson, pages 206–207.

Homework and Practice Book ■ 45

© Harcourt

Name _____ Date _____

Life in New England

DIRECTIONS Use the words in the box below to complete the sentences.

vote
praying
quilt-making
stocks
bartered

1. Puritans believed that reading the Bible and ___praying___ were the best ways to worship.

2. Several hours in the town ___stocks___ punished those who missed church.

3. Some Puritans enjoyed fishing and ___quilt-making___ .

4. Colonists sometimes ___bartered___ to meet their economic needs.

5. In the New England Colonies, only free white men who owned property could ___vote___ .

(continued)

46 ■ Homework and Practice Book

Use after reading Chapter 5, Lesson 2, pages 208–213.

© Harcourt

Homework and Practice Book Teacher Edition ■ 23

Name _____ Date _____

DIRECTIONS Read each numbered word or phrase. On the line provided, write the letter of the word or phrase that goes with it.

e **1** stocks   a. barrels
d **2** common   b. alphabet
c **3** sawmill   c. lumber
g **4** blacksmith   d. livestock
a **5** cooper   e. punishment
i **6** meetinghouse   f. butter
f **7** churn   g. iron tools
j **8** animal fat   h. brushes
h **9** pig hair   i. church
b **10** hornbook   j. soap

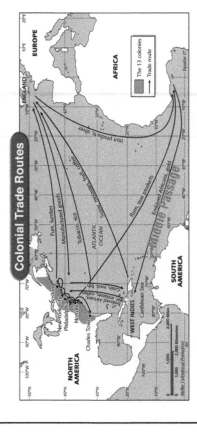

DIRECTIONS Answer the questions below.

1 What jobs did women and girls have?
Women and girls prepared and cooked food. They churned
butter and made clothing and household items.

2 What jobs did men and boys have?
Men and boys spent their days working in the fields and
hunting.

3 Why was education so important to the Puritans?
Puritans believed that everyone should know how to read so
that they could read the Bible.

Use after reading Chapter 5, Lesson 2, pages 208–213.   Homework and Practice Book ■ 47

Name _____ Date _____

New England's Economy

DIRECTIONS Use the map to help you answer the questions below.

Colonial Trade Routes

(map showing North America, South America, Europe, Africa, Atlantic Ocean, Caribbean Sea, with labels: NORTH AMERICA, SOUTH AMERICA, EUROPE, AFRICA, ENGLAND, WEST INDIES, Boston, New York City, Philadelphia, Norfolk, Charles Town, Middle Passage, Equator. Trade goods labeled: Iron products, silver; Furs, lumber; Manufactured goods; Tobacco, rice; Sugar, molasses, coffee; Rum, iron products; Enslaved Africans, gold; Grain, meat, fish; Enslaved Africans, sugar, molasses, coffee)

Legend: The 13 colonies; → Trade route

1 Which products did colonists export to Africa? rum, iron products

2 Besides enslaved Africans, what was brought from the West Indies to the colonies?
sugar, molasses, coffee

3 Which goods did the New England Colonies export to England? What did they get in return?
furs, lumber; manufactured goods

4 After English ships unloaded iron products and silver in Africa, what was loaded onto the ships? Where did they go next? They were loaded
with enslaved Africans and gold. Next, they sailed to the West
Indies.

5 On the map, label the route that is the Middle Passage.
See map.

48 ■ Homework and Practice Book   Use after reading Chapter 5, Lesson 3, pages 214–219.

© Harcourt

Chapter 5 · Study Guide

DIRECTIONS Fill in the missing information in these paragraphs about the New England Colonies. Use the terms below to help you complete the paragraphs for each lesson.

Lesson 1	Lesson 2	Lesson 3
charter	barter	exports
consent	common	imports
dissent	Harvard College	industries
expel	town meetings	free-market
sedition		naval stores

Lesson 1 The king of England gave the Puritans a **charter** to start the Massachusetts Bay Colony. The Puritan leaders were strict rulers who did not allow any **dissent**, or disagreement. It was common for the leaders to **expel** people who did not agree with them. One of those colonists expelled from the Massachusetts Bay Colony was a minister named Roger Williams. He started a new settlement based on the **consent** of the settlers. When Anne Hutchinson questioned their teachings, the leaders charged her with **sedition**.

(continued)

Lesson 2 The Puritans lived and worked together in small towns. At **town meetings**, they voted on laws and elected leaders. Only free white men who owned property could vote. To meet their economic needs, the Puritans would **barter** with each other. They all shared the **common**, which was used for grazing sheep, cattle, and other livestock. They also shared in the belief that learning to read was important. In 1636, the Puritans founded **Harvard College**.

Lesson 3 New England colonists created a **free-market** economy in which people are free to compete in business and set different prices for goods and services. The region's **industries** included logging and fishing. Some logs were used to make the **naval stores** needed to build ships. Trade was also an important part of the economy. **Exports** included furs, lumber, grain, whale oil, and dried fish. Most **imports**, or goods brought into the colonies, were English-made.

Name _____ Date _____

Settling the Middle Colonies

DIRECTIONS Read each description. Write its number on the map in the colony it describes. Also, fill in the blanks below each description with the name of the correct colony. One colony will be used twice.

The Middle Colonies

Lake Huron · Lake Erie · Lake Ontario

0 75 150 Miles
0 75 150 Kilometers
Albers Equal-Area Projection

N

ATLANTIC OCEAN

New York 4 5 1
Pennsylvania 3 2
New Jersey
Delaware

Middle Colonies
Present-day border

1 The first Quaker colony in North America was founded here.
New Jersey

2 William Penn was the proprietor of Pennsylvania and this colony.
Delaware

3 James, Duke of York, gave this land to John Berkeley and George Carteret.
New Jersey

4 William Penn's frame of government gave its citizens important rights.
Pennsylvania

5 Before its name was changed, it was the Dutch colony of New Netherland.
New York

© Harcourt

Use after reading Chapter 6, Lesson 1, pages 224–230.

Name _____ Date _____

Summarize the Chapter

SUMMARIZE

DIRECTIONS Complete this graphic organizer to show that you can summarize how the New England Colonies grew.

Key Fact

Possible response: As colonists spread across New England, they settled where Native Americans already lived and hunted.

Key Fact

Possible response: Puritans sent some of their crops to the English colonies in the Caribbean islands to trade for sugar.

Key Fact

Possible response: As a result of the many ships built in New England, trading became the center of the region's economy.

Summary

The New England Colonies grew during the 1600s.

Use after reading Chapter 5, pages 198–221.

© Harcourt

Name _____ Date _____

Life in the Middle Colonies

DIRECTIONS Read each sentence. If the sentence is true, write *T* on the line provided. If the sentence is false, write *F*.

F **1** Philadelphia grew slowly because not much was happening there.

T **2** The Middle Colonies were home to people of many different religions.

F **3** Dances and concerts were not popular in the Middle Colonies because most people believed that they were a waste of time.

T **4** Benjamin Franklin lived in Philadelphia and worked to improve the city.

T **5** Many immigrants to the Middle Colonies wanted the chance to make a new life and buy their own land.

T **6** William Penn designed Philadelphia with wide streets and many public parks.

(continued)

Use after reading Chapter 6, Lesson 2, pages 234–239. **Homework and Practice Book ▪ 53**

Name _____ Date _____

DIRECTIONS Imagine that you are George Whitefield and that you are being interviewed by a newspaper reporter. Answer the questions in the space provided.

1 What is the Great Awakening?
It is a religious movement that is changing the way many people practice their religion.

2 How are your sermons different from those of other ministers?
I tell people about having a direct relationship with God.

3 You are seen as one of the leaders of the movement. Who else is a leader in spreading these ideas?
Jonathan Edwards is another leader of our movement.

4 Why has your movement affected so many people?
We hold revivals at which everyone is welcome, including poor people, women, and Africans.

5 Your movement is not popular with all people. How has it affected religion in the colonies? Many people have joined churches. They feel that they have more freedom of religion.

54 ▪ Homework and Practice Book Use after reading Chapter 6, Lesson 2, pages 234–239.

Name _____ Date _____

Busy Farms and Seaports

DIRECTIONS Read each question, and choose the best answer. Then fill in the circle for the answer that you have chosen.

1. What happened at a gristmill?
   - Ⓐ Logs were made into lumber.
   - Ⓑ Iron was made into horseshoes.
   - Ⓒ Thread was made into cloth.
   - Ⓓ Grain was made into flour.

2. Which of the following did the Middle Colonies import from England?
   - Ⓐ grain
   - Ⓑ gunpowder
   - Ⓒ lumber
   - Ⓓ enslaved workers

3. Which of these workers could make finished goods from farm products?
   - Ⓐ blacksmiths
   - Ⓑ coopers
   - Ⓒ masons
   - Ⓓ bakers

4. What was the name for a young person who was learning a skill?
   - Ⓐ an apprentice
   - Ⓑ an artisan
   - Ⓒ a mason
   - Ⓓ a tanner

5. Which of the following was NOT important to the prosperity of the Middle Colonies?
   - Ⓐ farms
   - Ⓑ trade
   - Ⓒ whales
   - Ⓓ ports

(continued)

Name _____ Date _____

DIRECTIONS Choose the word or phrase from the box that best completes each sentence.

harbor	Delaware River	fur traders
market towns	skilled trades	silversmith shops

1. Farmers in the Middle Colonies traveled to __market towns__ to sell or trade their livestock and crops.

2. __Fur traders__ who lived inland floated their goods down rivers to port cities.

3. New York City had a __harbor__ along the East River that offered a good place for ships to dock.

4. Philadelphia grew with the help of its location on the __Delaware River__.

5. Some colonists made their living in __skilled trades__, such as carpentry and blacksmithing.

6. Women and girls had fewer chances to work outside the home. However, some women took over taverns, printing businesses, and __silversmith shops__ when their husbands died.

Skills: Make an Economic Choice

DIRECTIONS Making wise economic choices was an important skill for people living in the Middle Colonies. Most people could not buy everything they wanted at one time. Imagine that you are a farmer in the Middle Colonies. Complete the diagram.

You have grown enough grain to trade for one of the following:

A new, warmer winter coat

A plow that will save time in planting crops

If I buy the coat, I do not get
a plow.

The bad part of this choice is that
I will have to work more.

If I buy the plow, I do not get
a new coat.

The bad part of this choice is that
I will have to give up being
warm outside.

My choice is **Students may choose either the plow or the coat.**
Why did you make this choice? **Students should say why they thought
that one choice was better for them.**

Use after reading Chapter 6, Skill Lesson, pages 246–247.

Homework and Practice Book ■ 57

Chapter 6

Study Guide

DIRECTIONS Fill in the missing information in these paragraphs about the Middle Colonies. Use the terms below to help you complete the paragraph for each lesson.

Lesson 1	Lesson 2	Lesson 3
Tamanend	militia	apprentices
refuge	Great Awakening	tanners
James, Duke of York	immigrants	bricklayers
proprietor	Benjamin Franklin	artisans
Peter Stuyvesant	George Whitefield	prosperity

Lesson 1 The Middle Colonies had a diverse population. The Dutch colony of New Netherland was led by _____ **Peter Stuyvesant** _____.

The colony welcomed settlers from many countries. In 1664, _____ **James, Duke of York** _____, sent English warships to take New Netherland.

It became two English colonies, New York and New Jersey. Quakers found a _____ **refuge** _____ in New Jersey. William Penn was the _____ **proprietor** _____ of Pennsylvania and Delaware. He met with _____ **Tamanend** _____ and made peace with nearby Native Americans.

58 ■ Homework and Practice Book

Use after reading Chapter 6, pages 224–249.

(continued)

Homework and Practice Book Teacher Edition ■ 29

Summarize the Chapter

★ SUMMARIZE

DIRECTIONS Complete the graphic organizers to show that you can summarize facts about the Middle Colonies.

Key Fact
People came to the Middle Colonies from many places.

Key Fact
People had different backgrounds and religious beliefs.

Key Fact
There were many ways to make a living in the Middle Colonies.

Summary
The Middle Colonies had a lot of diversity. _____

Key Fact
Religious toleration rose in the Middle Colonies.

Key Fact
The diversity of religious beliefs became greater.

Key Fact
Freedom of religion grew.

Summary
The Great Awakening changed the religious life of the colonies.

Use after reading Chapter 6, pages 224–249.

Lesson 2 Philadelphia was an important city in the Middle Colonies. Many ___immigrants___ arrived there to start new lives. The city was home to many famous people. ___Benjamin Franklin___ helped start a fire department, a hospital, a library, and a college. He also organized a ___militia___ to protect the colony. In the 1720s, the ___Great Awakening___ changed the way many people practiced their religion. ___George Whitefield___ and other ministers spread their ideas throughout the Middle Colonies.

Lesson 3 The economy of the Middle Colonies was as diverse as the region's people. Farming and trade were the main reasons for the region's ___prosperity___. This economic success also created other kinds of jobs. ___Artisans___ used raw materials to make goods ranging from iron tools to barrels. ___Bricklayers___ used stone to pave streets and raise buildings. ___Tanners___ turned animal skins into leather for shoes. Young people learned these skills by becoming ___apprentices___.

Use after reading Chapter 6, pages 224–249.

Settling the South

DIRECTIONS Choose the correct term from the box to complete the chart.

as a safe place for Catholics	enslaved Africans
wealthy English family	the colony split into two
the Lords Proprietors	moved south to get more land
James Oglethorpe	1633
to give debtors a new start	English

SETTLING THE SOUTH

Where	Who	Why	When
Maryland	1. Founder: the Calverts, a **wealthy English family** First proprietor: Cecilius Calvert First governor: Leonard Calvert	2. **as a safe place for Catholics** and to make money	3. **1633**
Carolina	4. Founders: **the Lords Proprietors** 5. First colonists: English settlers, wealthy landowners from the West Indies, and **enslaved Africans**	6. **moved south to get more land**	7. founded 1663; in 1712: **the colony split into two**
Georgia	8. Founder: **James Oglethorpe** 9. First colonists: **English**	10. **to give debtors a new start**	1733

(continued)

DIRECTIONS Use the completed chart on page 61 to help you answer these questions.

1. Which colony was set up to help debtors?
Georgia

2. What happened in Carolina in 1712?
The colony was split into two.

3. Which colony did the Calverts found?
Maryland

4. Which group wanted religious freedom in Maryland?
Catholics

5. Who were the Lords Proprietors?
the leaders who founded Carolina

6. Which colony was founded 100 years after the Maryland Colony?
Georgia

7. Who were the Calverts?
a rich English family; the founders of Maryland

8. Where did many colonists settle as more people moved to Maryland and Virginia?
Carolina

9. Who founded the Georgia Colony? When was it founded?
James Oglethorpe; 1733

10. Which colony had settlers from the West Indies?
Carolina

James Oglethorpe

Skills: Compare Maps with Different Scales

DIRECTIONS Answer the questions below by choosing the map on page 64 that best answers the question.

1. Which map could you use to find the distance from Alexandria to Williamsburg?
   Map B

2. Which map could you use to find the distance between Henrico and Jamestown?
   Map A

3. Which map would you use to find the distance from Norfolk to Richmond? **Map B** Explain why.
   Possible response: The scale makes it easier to measure.

4. What is the distance between Norfolk and Richmond in miles?
   about 75 miles

5. Which map could you use to find the distance from Fredericksburg to Jamestown? **Map B** What is the distance in miles?
   about 75 miles

6. What is the distance in miles going due west from Norfolk to the Roanoke River **Map B**
   about 150 miles

7. Which map would you use to find the New River? **Map B**

8. Which map would you choose if you wanted to plan a trip from Newport News to Fredericksburg? **Map A**
   Why? **Map A shows Newport News and gives more detail.**

9. Which map would you choose if you were going to show someone where you wanted to start a settlement on Chesapeake Bay? **Map A**
   Explain why. **Map A shows the Chesapeake Bay in better detail.**

(continued)

Map A: Virginia Colony

VIRGINIA

Fredericksburg
Rappahannock River
James River
Richmond
Henrico
York River
Williamsburg
Jamestown
Newport News
Kecoughton
Norfolk
Cape Henry
Chesapeake Bay
ATLANTIC OCEAN
Roanoke River

0 20 40 Miles
0 20 40 Kilometers
Albers Equal-Area Projection

Map B: Virginia Colony

PENNSYLVANIA
NEW JERSEY
DELAWARE
MARYLAND
VIRGINIA
NORTH CAROLINA

Ohio River
Shenandoah River
Potomac River
Alexandria
Fredericksburg
Rappahannock River
James River
Richmond
York River
Jamestown
Williamsburg
Norfolk
Chesapeake Bay
ATLANTIC OCEAN
Roanoke River
New River

0 50 100 Miles
0 50 100 Kilometers
Albers Equal-Area Projection

The Southern Economy

DIRECTIONS Answer the questions below.

1 Which cash crop grew well on warm, wet land? __rice__

2 Why did the cash crop indigo help the Southern economy?
__Indigo grew well where rice did not.__

3 Besides agriculture and trade, what were two industries in the Southern
Colonies? __industry that produced forest products, industry that__
__produced naval stores__

4 What role did brokers play in the Southern economy? __Brokers took__
__the planters' crops to market to sell and brought back the goods__
__the planters wanted.__

5 How do you think enslaved African workers added to the economic success of
the Southern Colonies?
__Possible response: They did most of the work on plantations, which__
__grew the crops that brought cash into the Southern Colonies.__

Use after reading Chapter 7, Lesson 3, pages 268–271.

© Harcourt

Life in the South

DIRECTIONS Read the passage below. Use the information it contains to
complete the Venn diagram, comparing and contrasting life in the South.

Plantations and Small Farms

Many Southern colonists lived and worked on small farms. They planted and har-
vested their own crops. The owners of small farms did most of the work themselves. Few
of them owned slaves. Many families on small farms lived in one-story houses, far from
their neighbors.

People on plantations also lived far from others. However, many families lived on
plantation land. Some plantations looked like small villages, with many buildings circling
the owner's home. Some buildings were workshops where enslaved Africans made nails,
bricks, barrels, and other items used on the plantation. The kitchen was in a building
by itself. Plantation owners often lived in large houses. Many of the plantations in the
Southern Colonies ran themselves. Planters grew food, and skilled workers made needed
goods. Enslaved Africans did most of the work on the plantations.

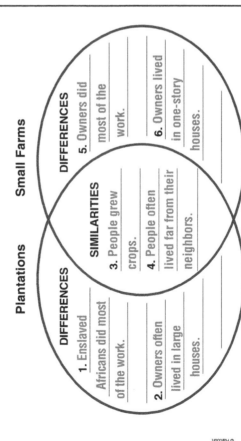

Plantations   **Small Farms**

DIFFERENCES

1. Enslaved
Africans did most
of the work.

2. Owners often
lived in large
houses.

SIMILARITIES

3. People grew
crops.

4. People often
lived far from their
neighbors.

DIFFERENCES

5. Owners did
most of the
work.

6. Owners lived
in one-story
houses.

Use after reading Chapter 7, Lesson 2, pages 262–266.

© Harcourt

Name _____ Date _____

Lesson 2 Most Southern colonists lived and worked on plantations

or on small farms. **Planters** were the richest

people in the colonies. They hired **overseers**

to watch enslaved workers in their fields. In time, slavery became

institutionalized , or a part of life. Some enslaved people

escaped from plantations. Those who went to live among the Seminole

in Florida were called **Black Seminoles** . Others started the

settlement of **Fort Mose** in Spanish Florida.

Lesson 3 Cash crops were important to the Southern economy.

Tobacco grew in Maryland, Virginia, and northern

North Carolina. Rice and **indigo** grew farther south.

In fact, rice was often called " **Carolina gold** ." Grain and

tobacco were shipped from Baltimore. **Shipbuilding** was

also an important industry in that city. **Wilmington** was an

important shipping center for forest goods.

Use after reading Chapter 7, pages 252–275.

Study Guide

DIRECTIONS Fill in the missing information in these paragraphs about the Southern Colonies. Use the terms below to help you complete the paragraph for each lesson.

Lesson 1	Lesson 2	Lesson 3
Maryland	Black Seminoles	shipbuilding
James Oglethorpe	overseers	Carolina gold
backcountry	Fort Mose	indigo
constitution	planters	tobacco
Toleration Act	institutionalized	Wilmington

Lesson 1 The Calvert family founded the **Maryland**

Colony along Chesapeake Bay. The colony's government passed the

Toleration Act , which gave religious freedom to all

Christians. The Lords Proprietors founded Carolina and adopted

a **constitution** , or plan of government, for it.

James Oglethorpe founded Georgia to offer a new life to

English debtors. In the mid-1700s, settlers began to move inland to a

region they called the **backcountry** .

(continued)

Use after reading Chapter 7, pages 252–275.

Name _____ Date _____

Summarize the Chapter

FOCUS SKILL: SUMMARIZE

DIRECTIONS Complete the graphic organizers to show that you can summarize facts about the Southern Colonies.

Key Fact
As the South grew, conflicts arose between settlers and Native Americans.

Key Fact
Many Africans were brought to southern plantations as enslaved workers.

Key Fact
The economy depended on cash crops grown on plantations.

Summary
Plantations were important to growth and the Southern economy.

Key Fact
Enslaved people often resisted slavery by breaking tools or working slowly.

Key Fact
Enslaved people kept their culture alive by telling stories and singing songs about Africa.

Key Fact
Christianity became a source of strength for some enslaved people.

Summary
Enslaved Africans dealt with the hardships of their lives in many ways.

Use after reading Chapter 7, pages 252–275.

Homework and Practice Book ▪ 69

© Harcourt

Name _____ Date _____

Fighting for Control

DIRECTIONS Number the sentences in the order in which the events happened.

Chief Pontiac

1 ⑥ To make up for Spain's losses, France gave Spain most of Louisiana.

2 ⑤ The British captured Fort Duquesne and several other French forts.

3 ⑦ The French and Indian War ended with the Treaty of Paris, giving Britain most of Canada, all French lands east of the Mississippi River, and Spanish Florida.

4 ⑨ King George III made the Proclamation of 1763. It said that all land west of the Appalachian Mountains belonged to the Native Americans.

5 3 Colonial leaders met to talk about how to deal with the French forces.

6 2 The French and Indian War began with the Battle of Fort Necessity.

7 1 The French sent soldiers to the Ohio Valley to drive British traders out.

8 10 The British Parliament passed the Sugar Act. It was designed to make colonists help pay for Britain's defense of the colonies.

9 8 Chief Pontiac united Native American tribes and captured British forts.

10 4 Benjamin Franklin's Albany Plan of Union was not approved.

70 ▪ Homework and Practice Book

Use after reading Chapter 8, Lesson 1, pages 294–299.

© Harcourt

Name _____ Date _____

Skills: Compare Historical Maps

DIRECTIONS Use the maps below to help you answer the questions that follow.

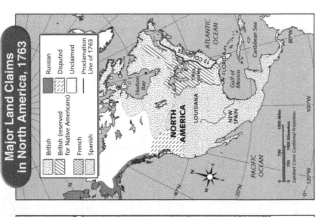

Major Land Claims in North America, 1754

Major Land Claims in North America, 1763

1 Which country claimed Louisiana in 1754?

France

2 Which countries gained land between 1754 and 1763?

Spain and Britain

Use after reading Chapter 8, Skill Lesson, pages 300–301.　　Homework and Practice Book ■ 71

(continued)

Name _____ Date _____

3 Which country lost all its lands in North America between 1754 and 1763?

France

4 Which event explains the differences between the two maps?

the French and Indian War

5 Which regions did Britain claim both in 1754 and in 1763?

land bordering the Atlantic Ocean and the land north of Louisiana and around Hudson Bay

6 What happened to Louisiana between 1754 and 1763?

It changed from French control to Spanish control.

7 Which two countries probably claimed land that bordered the disputed area of the Pacific Northwest in 1763?

Spain and Britain

8 For which group was the land in the Ohio Valley area reserved by King George III?

Native Americans

9 Which area changed from Spanish control in 1754 to British control in 1763?

Florida

10 Did any areas change from British control to Spanish control?

no

72 ■ Homework and Practice Book　　Use after reading Chapter 8, Skill Lesson, pages 300–301.

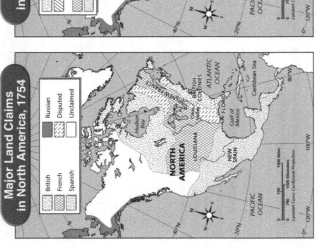

Name _____ Date _____

Disagreements Grow

DIRECTIONS Answer the following questions about the First Continental Congress.

1 Where did the First Continental Congress meet?

in Philadelphia

2 How did the First Continental Congress get its name?

It was the first meeting of its kind on the North American

continent.

3 What did the First Continental Congress do when it met?

It sent a signed request to the king.

4 In its signed petition to the king, which rights did the First Continental Congress claim colonists had?

the right to life and liberty, the right to assemble, and the right

to trial by jury

5 The First Continental Congress set what deadline for the British Parliament to respond?

May 10, 1775

6 How did the First Continental Congress make war with Britain more likely? It also

It asked the colonies to stop most trade with Britain. It also

asked the colonies to form militias.

   Use after reading Chapter 8, Lesson 3, pages 310–315.

Name _____ Date _____

Colonists Speak Out

DIRECTIONS Read each numbered description. On the line provided, write the letter of the person, group, or law that goes with it.

1 __f__ protested tax laws in Parliament

2 __e__ passed a tax on colonial newspapers

3 __a__ was accused of treason by others in the House of Burgesses

4 __b__ wrote plays about British leaders being greedy

5 __g__ captured British tax collectors

6 __c__ wove their own cloth

7 __h__ organized the first Committee of Correspondence in Boston

8 __j__ included a tax on imports to the colonies

9 __d__ was killed at the Boston Massacre

10 __i__ made a picture of the Boston Massacre

a. Patrick Henry

b. Mercy Otis Warren

c. Daughters of Liberty

d. Crispus Attucks

e. Stamp Act

f. Benjamin Franklin

g. Sons of Liberty

h. Samuel Adams

i. Paul Revere

j. Townshend Acts

Benjamin Franklin

Use after reading Chapter 8, Lesson 2, pages 302–308.

Name _____ Date _____

The Road to War

DIRECTIONS Choose the phrase from the box that best completes each sentence. Write the phrase in the blank.

Olive Branch Petition	Continental currency
Continental Army	Bunker Hill
Second Continental Congress	

1 The **Second Continental Congress** met after the fighting at Lexington and Concord.

2 The **Continental Army** differed from militias in that it was made up of mostly full-time soldiers.

3 To supply the Continental Army, Congress printed **Continental currency** .

4 The **Olive Branch Petition** asked Britain's King George III for peace.

5 After the Battle of **Bunker Hill** , the king promised to do whatever was necessary to crush the colonists' rebellion.

Use after reading Chapter 8, Lesson 4, pages 318–322.

Name _____ Date _____

Declaring Independence

DIRECTIONS Read each sentence below. On the line provided, write the name of the person that the sentence tells about.

John Adams	John Dickinson	John Hancock
Thomas Paine	Thomas Jefferson	Richard Henry Lee

1 "I told the Second Continental Congress that the 13 colonies no longer owed loyalty to the British king."
Richard Henry Lee

2 "I was the president of the Second Continental Congress and the first person to sign the Declaration of Independence."
John Hancock

3 "I was the main writer of the Declaration of Independence."
Thomas Jefferson

4 "I thought that Americans should always celebrate Independence Day."
John Adams

5 "I wrote *Common Sense*, which said that people should rule themselves."
Thomas Paine

6 "I headed the committee that wrote the Articles of Confederation."
John Dickinson

Use after reading Chapter 8, Lesson 5, pages 324–331.

Skills: Identify Multiple Causes and Effects

DIRECTIONS Using the chart below, answer the questions about causes and effects.

The Declaration of Independence

Causes

| Richard Henry Lee calls for a resolution stating that the colonies are independent. | → | Congress chooses a committee to write the Declaration of Independence. |

| Thomas Jefferson writes most of the Declaration of Independence. | | Congress approves the Declaration of Independence. |

Effects

| Crowds celebrate the colonies' independence. | → | The Declaration of Independence is read publicly for the first time. |

1 Which effect do you think first followed the causes? Why?
The writing of the Declaration of Independence. It had to be written before it could be read or approved.

2 Which effect showed how people felt about the Declaration of Independence?
Crowds celebrate the colonies' independence.

Chapter 8

Study Guide

DIRECTIONS Fill in the missing information in these paragraphs. Use the terms below to help you complete the paragraphs.

Lesson 1	Lesson 2	Lesson 3	Lesson 4	Lesson 5
proclamation	treason	monopoly	olive branch	grievances
alliances	imperial policies	blockade	commander	independence
delegates	boycott	petition	in chief	resolution
	representation		earthworks	

Lesson 1 In the French and Indian War, Britain and France fought over land claims in North America. Both sides made **alliances** with Native Americans. At a meeting in Albany, New York, Benjamin Franklin asked the British colonies to join together to fight the French. The **delegates** did not approve his plan. After Britain won the war, its king made a **proclamation** that set aside certain lands for Native Americans.

Lesson 2 The French and Indian War was costly for Britain. Britain decided to tax colonists to raise money. Many colonists said that Parliament could not tax them because the colonists had no **representation**, or voice, in Parliament. When Patrick Henry argued that colonists should not pay, some people accused him of **treason**. Many others agreed with Henry, though. More and more colonists began to **boycott** British goods and protest Britain's **imperial policies**. Fights broke out as colonists protested new taxes.

(continued)

Homework and Practice Book Teacher Edition ▪ 39

Name _____ Date _____

Summarize the Chapter

⭐ CAUSE AND EFFECT

DIRECTIONS Complete this graphic organizer to show that you you understand the causes and effects of events leading to the American Revolution.

Cause	→	Effect
Britain needed money to pay for the French and Indian War.	→	**Possible response:** Parliament passed the Sugar Act.
Possible response: Americans wanted to be independent from Britain.	→	Congress approves the Declaration of Independence.
Britain passed the Intolerable Acts.	→	**Possible response:** The colonies sent representatives to the First Continental Congress.
Fights between British soldiers and colonists often broke out.	→	**Possible response:** The Boston Massacre took place.

Use after reading Chapter 8, pages 294–335.

© Harcourt

Name _____ Date _____

Lesson 3 The Tea Act gave Britain a __monopoly__ on tea in the colonies. In response, the Sons of Liberty threw boxes of British tea into Boston Harbor. British leaders were so angry that they ordered the British navy to __blockade__ the harbor. Colonial leaders met at the First Continental Congress and decided to send a __petition__ to the king, stating colonists' rights.

Lesson 4 The Second Continental Congress set up the Continental Army and named George Washington its __commander in chief__. The war's first major battle had already taken place at Lexington and Concord. At Breed's Hill, colonists fired at British soldiers from defenses called __earthworks__. The British won the Battle at Breed's Hill, mistakenly called the Battle of Bunker Hill. However, more than 1,000 British soldiers died. Congress later asked King George III for peace. Its petition was named after the __olive branch__, an ancient symbol of peace.

Lesson 5 Conflicts between Britain and the colonies grew, and more and more colonists wanted __independence__ from Britain. In Congress, Richard Henry Lee called for a __resolution__ to free the colonies. Congress chose a committee to write a declaration to King George III. This statement became known as the Declaration of Independence. It listed many __grievances__, or complaints, that the colonists had against the king and Parliament.

Use after reading Chapter 8, pages 294–335.

Homework and Practice Book ■ 79

© Harcourt

Name _____ Date _____

Americans and the Revolution

DIRECTIONS Read each statement below. On the line provided, write *P* if the statement is something that a Patriot would have said. Write *L* if the statement is something that a Loyalist would have said. Write *N* if it is something that a neutral person would have said.

P ❶ "I never thought I would burn my own crops, but it's better than giving food to redcoats."

N ❷ "I don't care who wins. I just want this war to end."

L ❸ "The soldiers have a right to take what they need from rebels."

L ❹ "I do not understand why my son has chosen to fight on the side of people who betray their king."

P ❺ "People who profiteer are traitors to the cause of freedom."

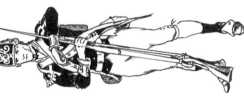

Use after reading Chapter 9, Lesson 1, pages 338–343.   Homework and Practice Book ▪ 81

Name _____ Date _____

Skills: Read Parallel Time Lines

DIRECTIONS Use the time lines to answer the questions.

America and the Revolution

| 1770 | 1775 | 1780 | 1785 |

1774 The First Continental Congress meets

1775 The Battles of Lexington and Concord are fought

1776 The Declaration of Independence is signed

1778 The colonies sign a treaty with France

1781 Americans force British to surrender at Yorktown, the last major battle of the war

France and the Revolution

| 1770 | 1775 | 1780 | 1785 |

1774 King Louis XV dies. His grandson, Louis XVI, becomes king

1777 Marquis de Lafayette and his forces arrive to help colonists fight the British

1778 France signs a treaty with the colonies

1780 French soldiers arrive at Newport, Rhode Island

1781 French soldiers help Continental Army surround Yorktown, site of the last major battle of the war

1781 French navy keeps fresh troops and supplies from reaching the British, and it brings more troops to aid Americans at Yorktown

❶ Who was the king of France during the Revolutionary War? __Louis XVI__

❷ When did the Marquis de Lafayette arrive in the colonies? __1777__

❸ Which event appears on both time lines? __the signing of a treaty between France and the colonies__

❹ Did the first French troops arrive in the colonies before or after the Declaration of Independence was signed? __after__

(continued)

82 ▪ **Homework and Practice Book**   Use after reading Chapter 9, Skill Lesson, pages 344–345.

Homework and Practice Book Teacher Edition ▪ 41

Fighting for Independence

DIRECTIONS Place each name from the box where it belongs on the chart.

John Burgoyne
Friedrich Wilhelm von Steuben
George Washington
Benedict Arnold
Jorge Farragut

Bernardo de Gálvez
William Howe
Marquis de Lafayette
George Clinton
Benjamin Franklin

Helped the Americans	Helped the British
Bernardo de Gálvez	John Burgoyne
Friedrich Wilhelm von Steuben	William Howe
George Washington	
Marquis de Lafayette	
Benedict Arnold	
George Clinton	
Jorge Farragut	
Benjamin Franklin	

(continued)

Use after reading Chapter 9, Lesson 2, pages 346–352.

---

5. Which time line shows the earliest battles in the war?

   America and the Revolution

6. Which was signed first, the treaty with France or the Declaration of Independence?

   the Declaration of Independence

7. Where did French troops arrive first, in Newport or in Yorktown?

   in Newport

List three ways in which the French helped bring about the British surrender at Yorktown.

8. **Possible response: The French navy kept the British from getting**

   fresh troops and supplies.

9. **Possible response: French ships brought soldiers to help the**

   Americans.

10. **Possible response: French soldiers helped Americans circle**

    Yorktown.

Use after reading Chapter 9, Skill Lesson, pages 344–345.

Name _____ Date _____

Winning Independence

Winning Independence

DIRECTIONS Follow the instructions below. Complete the activity by placing your answers on the map or by writing your answers on the lines provided.

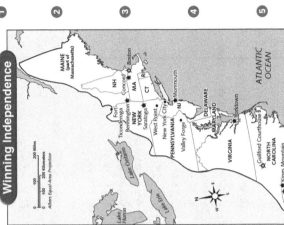

1 Draw an X at the city where Nathan Hale died.
New York City

2 Draw a pitcher at the battle where Mary Ludwig Hays McCauley took water to soldiers.
Monmouth

3 Draw a hammer next to the place where Tadeusz Kosciuszko planned a fort.
West Point

4 Circle the place where Nathanael Greene and Daniel Morgan led Americans to victory.
Cowpens

5 Draw a star next to the place where General Cornwallis gave up.
Yorktown

6 Underline the place where the only major battle was fought in North Carolina during the Revolutionary War.
Guilford Courthouse

Use after reading Chapter 9, Lesson 3, pages 356–361.

Name _____ Date _____

DIRECTIONS Use phrases from the paragraph below to complete the Venn diagram. Write each phrase in the correct section of the diagram.

The soldiers in both the Continental Army and the British army carried muskets with bayonets into battle, but these armies were very different. The British army had 50,000 experienced soldiers in the colonies. They were also helped by mercenaries. The Continental Army was made up of fewer than 15,000 soldiers. Many of these soldiers were farmers who had just signed up for the army. The armies also looked different and carried different things with them. The Continental soldier often wore a tricorn hat and carried a cartridge bag with a sling. The British soldier wore a bright red coat and carried a haversack for food.

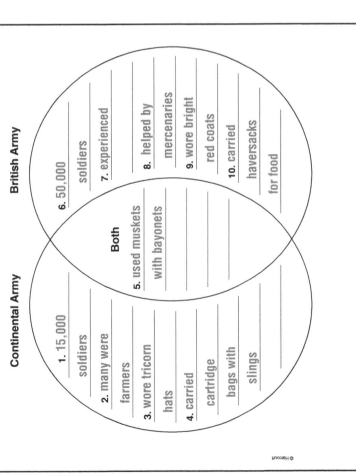

Continental Army

1. 15,000 soldiers
2. many were farmers
3. wore tricorn hats
4. carried cartridge bags with slings

Both

5. used muskets with bayonets

British Army

6. 50,000 soldiers
7. experienced
8. helped by mercenaries
9. wore bright red coats
10. carried haversacks for food

Use after reading Chapter 9, Lesson 2, pages 346–352.

Name _____ Date _____

Skills: Tell Fact from Fiction

DIRECTIONS Read the passages below about General Washington's crossing of the Delaware River. Then answer the questions.

Passage A   "As the four boys sat huddled together, the oarsmen dressed in tattered blue and buff uniforms used their long poles to push off the ice. Matt recognized them from the history report he and Q had worked on together.

"'They must be John Glover's Marbleheaders!' he whispered to Q.

"'This must be the Delaware River,' Q whispered back. Both boys remembered reading about the special group of seafaring enlisted men from the north, under the guidance of Colonel John Glover of Marblehead, Massachusetts. They had manned the sturdy Durham boats that had carried Washington and his troops across the river on that Christmas night.'"*

*Elvira Woodruff. *George Washington's Socks*. Scholastic, 1991.

Passage B   "I am sitting in the ferry house. The troops are all over, and boats have gone back for the artillery. We are three hours behind the set time . . . [the Marblehead fishermen] directing the boats have had a hard time to force boats through the floating ice with the snow drifting in their faces . . .'"*

*excerpt from *The Diary of Colonel John Fitzgerald* in *The American Revolution in the Delaware Valley* by Edward S. Gifford, Jr. Pennsylvania Society of Sons of the Revolution, 1976.

1 Which passage is from a documentary source?
   Passage B

2 Which passage is from a fictional source?
   Passage A

3 What is one clue that helped you make your decision?
   Possible response: The boys in Passage A knew who the
   fishermen were from their history report. That tells the reader that
   the boys are students who have traveled back in time.

Name _____ Date _____

Effects of the War

DIRECTIONS Read each question, and choose the best answer. Then fill in the circle for the answer that you have chosen.

1 Which idea in the Declaration of Independence changed people's views of slavery?
   (A) the idea that people must obey the government
   (B) the idea that all people have a right to life and liberty
   (C) the idea that the colonies would no longer be ruled by Britain
   (D) the idea that people should not be taxed without their consent

2 What argument did Elizabeth Freeman use to win her freedom in court?
   (A) She argued that all people are born equal.
   (B) She argued that her owner was cruel.
   (C) She argued that slavery had been abolished.
   (D) She argued that she had a right to vote.

3 Who formed the nation's first abolitionist group?
   (A) enslaved workers
   (B) Native Americans
   (C) planters
   (D) Quakers

4 Which state was the first to abolish slavery?
   (A) Georgia
   (B) Maryland
   (C) Massachusetts
   (D) Virginia

5 What did the Northwest Ordinance say about slavery?
   (A) It allowed slavery in the Northwest Territory.
   (B) It said slavery would not be allowed in states formed from the Northwest Territory.
   (C) It said that each state in the Northwest Territory could decide whether to allow slavery.
   (D) It did not mention slavery.

Chapter 9 Study Guide

DIRECTIONS Fill in the missing information in these paragraphs about the American Revolution. Use the names and terms below to help you complete the paragraphs.

Lesson 1	Lesson 2	Lesson 3	Lesson 4
Sybil Ludington	turning point	Nathan Hale	abolitionists
Thayendanegea	mercenaries	Benedict Arnold	ordinance
Peter Salem	negotiate	John Paul Jones	territories
James Armistead	campaign		
Deborah Sampson			

Lesson 1 The Revolutionary War affected nearly everyone in the colonies. Women played important roles in the war. Sixteen-year-old **Sybil Ludington** rode to tell Americans of a British attack. **Deborah Sampson** pretended to be a man and fought in the war. **James Armistead** African Americans also fought for the Patriots. won his freedom by working as a spy for George Washington. **Peter Salem** and several other African Americans fought at Concord. Native American groups formed alliances with both the Americans and the British. **Thayendanegea** and the Mohawk fought on the side of the British. The Oneida and Tuscarora fought for the Americans.

(continued)

Lesson 2 In 1777, the British began a **campaign** to capture New York. The large British army was helped by **mercenaries** from Germany. Yet the British lost an important battle at Saratoga. This battle was a **turning point** in the war. Benjamin Franklin had gone to France to **negotiate** with the French government. He wanted France to help Americans in the war. The American victory at Saratoga convinced French leaders that colonists could win the war. The leaders agreed to help.

Lesson 3 The American Revolution created many strong leaders. **Nathan Hale** was a Patriot spy who was captured by the British and hanged. Navy commander **John Paul Jones** fought the British navy off the coast of Britain. The Revolution also made a few traitors. **Benedict Arnold**, who had led American troops to victory at Saratoga, turned against his country and led attacks on Virginia towns.

Lesson 4 State constitutions written after 1776 used the ideals of the American Revolution. The rights stated in the Declaration of Independence changed the way many people thought about people's rights and about slavery. Some people became **abolitionists** and spoke out against slavery. The slavery debate affected **territories** outside the states. In 1787, an **ordinance** governing lands in the Northwest Territory said that slavery would not be allowed in the region.

The Constitutional Convention

DIRECTIONS Write one or two sentences about each leader listed below. Name a contribution that the leader made to the Constitutional Convention.

1 James Madison

Possible response: He argued that the country needed to replace the Articles of Confederation.

2 Edmund Randolph

Possible response: He introduced the Virginia Plan. Under the plan, the number of representatives of each state would be based on the state's populations.

3 William Paterson

Possible response: Paterson offered the New Jersey Plan. In it, each state would be equally represented.

4 Roger Sherman

Possible response: He presented the Connecticut Compromise. It was the start of the Great Compromise.

5 Gouverneur Morris

Possible response: He spoke out against slavery, even after the Three-Fifths Compromise.

Use after reading Chapter 10, Lesson 1, pages 388–394.

© Harcourt

Summarize the Chapter

⭐ FOCUS SKILL CAUSE AND EFFECT

DIRECTIONS Complete this graphic organizer to show that you you understand the causes and effects of some of the key events of the **Revolutionary War.**

Cause		Effect
Congress printed more money.	→	The money became less valuable.
News of the American victory at Saratoga reached France.	→	France agreed to help the Americans.
The Treaty of Paris was signed.	→	Borders were set for a new country known as the United States of America.

Use after reading Chapter 9, pages 336–371.

© Harcourt

Name _____ Date _____

Three Branches of Government

DIRECTIONS Use the words and phrases in the box to complete the diagram.

Supreme Court	President	Senate	Executive Branch

Legislative Branch
- Senate
- House of Representatives

Executive Branch
- President
- Vice President

Judicial Branch
- Supreme Court
- District Courts

DIRECTIONS Read the list below of jobs in the government. In the space provided, write a brief description of the duties of the jobs.

1 Representatives

Representatives can make laws to manage conflict, raise an army and a navy, declare war, and coin and print money. They also control trade.

2 President

The President can veto bills, is commander in chief of the military, and carries out the nation's laws faithfully.

3 Supreme Court justices

Justices decide cases dealing with the Constitution, treaties, or national law. They also decide cases between states and between citizens of different states.

94 ■ Homework and Practice Book   Use after reading Chapter 10, Lesson 2, pages 398–403.

Name _____ Date _____

Skills: Resolve Conflict

DIRECTIONS Complete the graphic organizer below. For each step, write the decisions that led to the creation of the Constitution.

Identify the problem.

1 Delegates argued over how the states would be represented in Congress.

Have both sides explain what they want.

2 Bigger states wanted representation based on population. Smaller states wanted the same number of representatives in each state.

Think of possible compromises. Choose one.

3 Edmund Randolph introduced the Virginia Plan. William Paterson offered the New Jersey Plan. Delegates agreed on the Great Compromise.

Try the compromise.

4 The Great Compromise settled the argument and was passed on July 16, 1787. The delegates kept working on the Constitution.

Use after reading Chapter 10, Skill Lesson, pages 396–397.   Homework and Practice Book ■ 93

Homework and Practice Book Teacher Edition ■ 47

Left panel (page 95)

Name _____ Date _____

The Bill of Rights

DIRECTIONS Complete the diagram to show the freedoms promised by the First Amendment.

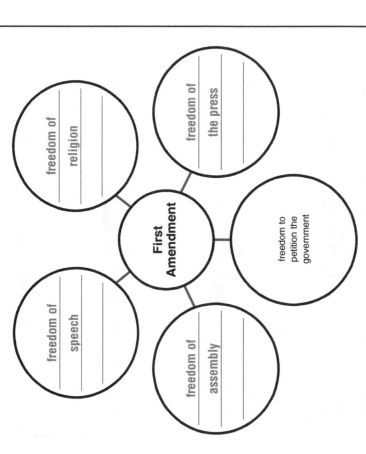

- freedom of religion
- freedom of the press
- freedom of speech
- freedom of assembly
- freedom to petition the government
- **First Amendment**

DIRECTIONS Write a sentence telling one way in which people today express one of these freedoms.

Possible response: People express freedom of the press by publishing their opinions in newspapers.

(continued)

Use after reading Chapter 10, Lesson 3, pages 404–409.

Homework and Practice Book ■ 95

© Harcourt

Right panel (page 96)

Name _____ Date _____

DIRECTIONS Next to each numbered item, write the letter of the correct description.

_f_ **1** Second Amendment

_c_ **2** Third Amendment

_d_ **3** Fourth Amendment

_a_ **4** Fifth Amendment, Sixth Amendment, Seventh Amendment, Eighth Amendment

_e_ **5** Ninth Amendment

_b_ **6** Tenth Amendment

a. Due process of law is promised.

b. The government can only do things listed in the Constitution.

c. The government cannot make people house soldiers.

d. It protects people against unfair searches of their homes.

e. People have rights aside from the ones listed in the Constitution.

f. It protects people's right to have weapons.

Use after reading Chapter 10, Lesson 3, pages 404–409.

© Harcourt

Skills: Read a Population Map

DIRECTIONS Use the map to help you answer the questions on page 98.

United States Population Density

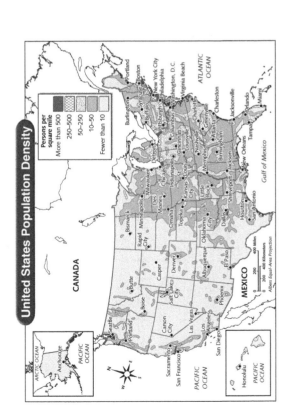

Persons per square mile
- More than 500
- 250–500
- 50–250
- 10–50
- Fewer than 10

(continued)

---

1 Which is more densely populated, the area around Burlington or the area around Charlotte? **the area around Charlotte**

2 What is the population density of the Virginia Beach area? **10–50 persons per square mile**

3 What is the population density in the United States of most of the area bordering Mexico? **fewer than 10 persons per square mile**

4 What are the most densely populated parts of California? **areas around cities on the south and central coasts—Los Angeles, San Francisco, and San Diego**

5 Which part of the country has the higher population density, the East or the West? **the East**

6 Which region of the country has the higher population density, the Great Lakes region or the Pacific Northwest region? **the Great Lakes region**

7 Which state has the lowest population density? **Alaska**

8 What is the population density where you live? **Answers will vary.** Place an X on the map to mark the location.

9 What is the population density of the area surrounding where you live? **Answers will vary.** Place a circle around the X to mark this area.

Name _____ Date _____

A Constitutional Democracy

DIRECTIONS Answer the questions in the space provided.

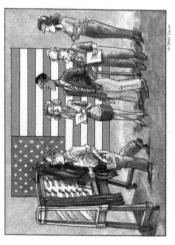

1 What are checks and balances?

They are powers that allow the three branches of government to watch over each other. They keep any one branch from becoming too powerful or misusing its authority.

2 How can Congress pass a law that the President has vetoed?

Congress can check the President's power by voting to override the veto with a two-thirds vote.

3 List three things state governments do.

They build highways and parks. They oversee public schools. They help citizens.

4 Who is the executive of a local government?

the mayor

5 What is one of a citizen's responsibilities?

voting

© Harcourt

Name _____ Date _____

Chapter 10 Study Guide

DIRECTIONS Fill in the missing information in these paragraphs about the Constitution. Use the terms and names below to help you complete the paragraphs.

Lesson 1	Lesson 2	Lesson 3	Lesson 4
convention	impeach	Anti-Federalists	governor
Daniel Shays	veto	bill of rights	local
James Madison	amendments	political parties	checks and balances
Patrick Henry	justices	ratify	popular sovereignty
Great Compromise	representatives	Federalists	mayor

Lesson 1 In 1787, __Daniel Shays__ and other protesters tried to take over a government arsenal in Massachusetts. This event told leaders that the nation needed a stronger government. __James Madison__ wanted to replace the Articles of Confederation. Other leaders, including __Patrick Henry__, wanted to keep the Articles. Still, 12 states sent delegates to a __convention__ in Philadelphia to fix the Articles of Confederation. The convention tried to come up with a way to represent each state. Although the delegates disagreed about slavery, the convention agreed on the __Great Compromise__ in 1787.

Lesson 2 Each branch of government limits the power of the other branches. For example, the President can __veto__, or reject, bills that __representatives__ in Congress pass. Congress can __impeach__ the President. The President nominates Supreme Court __justices__. The Constitution also explains the process for adding __amendments__, or changes.

(continued)

© Harcourt

Summarize the Chapter

DRAW CONCLUSIONS

DIRECTIONS Complete the graphic organizers to show that you can draw conclusions about the Constitution.

Evidence

The delegates set up a system of checks and balances.

Knowledge

Unchecked government may become too powerful.

Conclusion

The delegates to the Constitutional Convention did not want any one government branch to become too powerful.

Evidence

Delegates who supported the Constitution needed nine states to approve it.

Knowledge

People sometimes have to compromise to get what they want.

Conclusion

Delegates who supported the Constitution had to compromise so they could win its approval.

Lesson 3 The Constitution was completed in 1787. The delegates had to _____ratify_____ it, but some were worried. They wanted a limited government in which the Constitution would limit the power of the federal government and protect people's individual rights.

Supporters of the Constitution promised to propose a _____bill of rights_____ once the Constitution was approved. They were called _____Federalists_____. People who disagreed with them were called _____Anti-Federalists_____. This was the beginning of _____political parties_____. In 1791, the Bill of Rights became part of the Constitution.

Lesson 4 The Constitution grants powers to each branch of government. The branches have powers that allow them to watch over each other, called _____checks and balances_____. These powers make sure any one branch does not become too powerful.

The same three branches exist in state and _____local_____ governments. Powers that the states do not have are listed in the Constitution. State governments are led by a _____governor_____, and local governments are led by a _____mayor_____. The idea that governments get their power from the people is called _____popular sovereignty_____.

Name _____ Date _____

DIRECTIONS Below is a fictional letter from a member of the Corps of Discovery to a friend back home. Use the words and phrases in the box to complete the letter.

Rocky Mountains	Meriwether Lewis	Missouri River
Sacagawea	Thomas Jefferson	St. Louis
Pacific Ocean	William Clark	horses
Fort Mandan		

Dear Elizabeth,

Wonderful news! We have begun our journey home, and we hope to return to __St. Louis__ before autumn.

After we left there, we spent the winter of 1804–1805 along the __Missouri River__. We built a camp and named it __Fort Mandan__. In this same place, we met a Shoshone Indian woman who helped us greatly. Her name was __Sacagawea__, and she guided us safely through the lands of her people. She helped us buy __horses__, which we used to cross the __Rocky Mountains__. Then we built boats and rowed down several rivers, including the Columbia River. In November 1805, we finally reached the __Pacific Ocean__.

Our expedition succeeded because of our skilled leaders, __Meriwether Lewis__ and __William Clark__. They made maps of our journey and also collected seeds, plants, and animals to show President __Thomas Jefferson__. I know he will be glad that he persuaded Congress to pay for our trip.

I am eager to see you and hear your news.

Yours truly,
John

Use after reading Chapter 11, Lesson 1, pages 426–432.

© Harcourt

Name _____ Date _____

Exploring the West

DIRECTIONS Study the map. Read each statement. Choose the right name from the box, and write it on the line provided on the map.

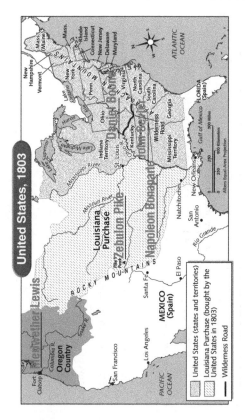

United States, 1803

Legend:
- United States (states and territories)
- Louisiana Purchase (bought by the United States in 1803)
- Wilderness Road

| John Sevier |
| Zebulon Pike |
| Daniel Boone |
| Meriwether Lewis |
| Napoleon Bonaparte |

1. I was one of the best-known pioneers to cross the Appalachians to reach Kentucky.

2. I was the first governor of Tennessee.

3. I sold this huge area to the United States for $15 million.

4. I spent the winter of 1805 here with the Corps of Discovery.

5. This tall mountain peak is named for me.

(continued)

Use after reading Chapter 11, Lesson 1, pages 426–432.

© Harcourt

Make a Thoughtful Decision

DIRECTIONS Imagine you are leading an expedition that is looking for a route to the Pacific coast. You want to travel west by river, but you do not know this river well. Follow the steps below to decide on a course of action.

Step 1 *Make a list of choices to help you reach your goal.*

1 I could try to lead the expedition on the river.

2 I could turn back and try to find another route west.

Step 2 *Gather information you will need to make a good decision.*

3 Possible response: I will watch to see if there are other boats traveling the river.

4 Possible response: I will send scouts on the river to take measurements of the river's current and depth.

5 Possible response: I will check to make sure that we have the supplies that we will need to make rafts.

Step 3 *Predict consequences, and compare them.*

6 Possible response: If the river is too difficult to travel, we will have wasted time building rafts and trying to travel it.

7 Possible response: If we turn back, we will be moving away from the Pacific coast, which is our goal.

Step 4 *Make a choice, and take action.*

8 Possible response: I will try to lead the expedition on the river. I will give the order to start building rafts.

Tell why you made the choice you made.

9 Possible response: I want to lead the expedition toward its goal.

Expanding Borders

DIRECTIONS Look at the time line. Match each description below with the correct dot on the time line. Write the correct number of the event in the space provided.

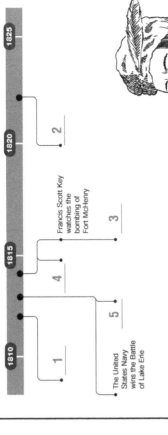

Tecumseh

Francis Scott Key watches the bombing of Fort McHenry — **3**

The United States Navy wins the Battle of Lake Erie — **5**

1   **4**   **2**

1 The United States declares war on Britain

2 The Monroe Doctrine is announced

3 The United States and Britain sign a peace treaty

4 British troops capture Washington, D.C., and burn the White House

5 American troops win the Battle of the Thames; Chief Tecumseh is killed

---

Name _____ Date _____

From Ocean to Ocean

DIRECTIONS Study the map and map key. Answer the questions.

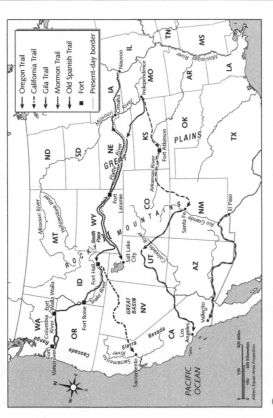

Map key:
→ Oregon Trail
⋯→ California Trail
→ Gila Trail
→ Mormon Trail
→ Old Spanish Trail
■ Fort
— Present-day border

1. What was the name of the trail that ended in present-day Utah?
Mormon Trail

2. Many people took the Oregon Trail west. In what city did this trail begin?
Independence, MO

3. What was the name of the trail that connected Fort Hall and Sacramento?
California Trail

4. Which present-day states did the Old Spanish Trail pass through?
New Mexico, Colorado, Utah, Nevada, and California

5. How many forts can you find on the map? Why do you think they are located along rivers? **Six; possible response: People and goods may have traveled to and from the forts by river; rivers provided water resources.**

(continued)

Use after reading Chapter 11, Lesson 3, pages 444–451.   Homework and Practice Book ■ **107**

Name _____ Date _____

DIRECTIONS Read each question, and write your answer in the space provided.

1. What were the groups of covered wagons called?
wagon trains

2. About how long did it take to travel to the Oregon Territory?
6 months

3. Why did people walk most of the way on their journey?
The wagons were filled with supplies.

4. What was manifest destiny?
the idea that the nation was meant to stretch from the Atlantic Ocean to the Pacific Ocean

5. Which river did the United States claim was the border between Texas and Mexico? Which river did Mexico claim was the border?
the Rio Grande; the Nueces River

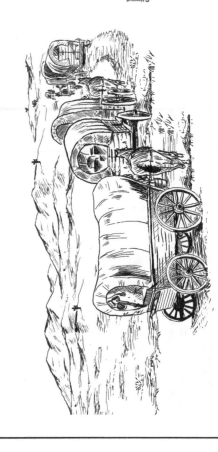

© Harcourt

New Ideas and Inventions

DIRECTIONS Read each statement and the names that appear in the box. On the line provided, write the name of the person or thing described.

canal	Industrial Revolution	mill
cotton gin	lock	reaper
Erie Canal	locomotive	steam engine
goods		

1 A __canal__ is a human-made waterway that connects bodies of water.

2 A __lock__ raises and lowers the boat to the level of the water in the next lock.

3 The __Erie Canal__ linked the Great Lakes to the Atlantic Ocean.

4 Robert Fulton used a __steam engine__ to power his boat, the *Clermont*.

5 The first American __locomotive__ was called the *Tom Thumb*.

6 The __Industrial Revolution__ is the name given to the new inventions and forms of transportation that changed the way people lived and worked.

7 During the 1800s, workers could make __goods__ more quickly and at a lower cost.

8 Francis Cabot Lowell built a __mill__ in Waltham, Massachusetts, that made raw cotton into finished cloth.

9 Eli Whitney invented the __cotton gin__, a machine that could quickly remove seeds.

10 Cyrus McCormick invented a mechanical __reaper__ for harvesting grain.

Chapter 11

Chapter Study Guide

DIRECTIONS Fill in the missing information in these paragraphs about frontier life. Use the terms below to help you complete the paragraphs.

Lesson 1	Lesson 2	Lesson 3	Lesson 4
Daniel Boone	Andrew Jackson	Mormon Trail	cotton gin
Cumberland	settlers	Texas	steamboats
Louisiana Purchase	Fort McHenry	Great Salt Lake	locomotives
Meriwether Lewis	James Madison	Alamo	inventions
Wilderness Road	Tecumseh	gold	canals

Lesson 1 One way over the Appalachians was on an old Native American trail that went through the __Cumberland__ Gap. __Daniel Boone__, an early pioneer, blazed a trail through the gap. It became known as the __Wilderness Road__, and it became the main route to the West. In 1803, Thomas Jefferson made the __Louisiana Purchase__, which more than doubled the size of the United States. Because little was known about the land, Jefferson chose __Meriwether Lewis__ and William Clark to explore the region.

Lesson 2 One problem leading to the War of 1812 was the __settlers__ who moved to lands that belonged to Native Americans. Chief __Tecumseh__ urged the different tribes to unite to stop them. In 1812, __James Madison__ asked Congress to declare war on Britain in 1812. In 1814, Francis Scott Key watched British ships bomb __Fort McHenry__ and wrote a poem that later became the national anthem. After the war, President __Andrew Jackson__ signed the Indian Removal Act, forcing the Cherokee and other tribes to leave their land.

(continued)

Summarize the Chapter

(★FOCUS Skill) DRAW CONCLUSIONS

DIRECTIONS Complete the graphic organizers to draw conclusions about the western expansion of the United States.

Evidence

Today, the United States stretches from the Atlantic Ocean to the Pacific Ocean.

Knowledge

The Louisiana Purchase and the Mexican-American War gave the United States many new lands.

Conclusion

Many people wanted to achieve manifest destiny.

Evidence

Americans and immigrants from other countries moved west to start new settlements.

Knowledge

The journeys were hard, long, and dangerous.

Conclusion

People were willing to risk their lives for the chance to own land, have religious freedom, and form their own settlements.

Lesson 3 The mid-nineteenth century was a time of major western settlement. Mexico's leaders wanted more settlers to move to Mexico, so they offered land in **Texas** to encourage setters. As more Americans arrived, the Mexican government tried to stop further settlement. This led to a battle at the **Alamo** . Instead, Americans followed the Oregon Trail west in covered wagons. Brigham Young led a group of Mormons on a 1,000-mile trip from Illinois to the **Great Salt Lake** , which became known as the **Mormon Trail** . In 1848, the discovery of **gold** in California changed the region forever.

Lesson 4 New **inventions** during the first half of the 1800s allowed people to travel and transport goods more easily. **Canals** connected bodies of water. **Steamboats** became the main form of travel on large rivers. Steam engines were also used in **locomotives** , or railroad engines. Eli Whitney's invention of the **cotton gin** greatly changed plantation farming.

The North and the South

DIRECTIONS Read the passage below. Then answer the questions in the space provided.

The North and the South could not agree about slavery. Most Northerners did not think that slavery should spread to the western territories. Most Southerners thought they had the right to take their enslaved workers west with them.

The Northern economy relied more on manufacturing and shipping. Agriculture was not as important to its economy as to the South's economy. Northern states did not need the same kinds of workers as the South did.

Many Northerners thought that slavery was wrong and should be abolished, or done away with. Those Northerners were called abolitionists. Even most Northerners who were not abolitionists did not want more slave states added to the country.

However, the economy of the South depended on enslaved workers. Plantation owners were able to harvest more cotton, indigo, and tobacco by using enslaved workers to work in the fields. Those Southerners believed that each state had the right to decide whether people could have enslaved workers.

❶ Compare the economies of the North and the South.
North: relied more on manufacturing and shipping
South: depended on agriculture; needed lots of enslaved workers

❷ How did many people in the North and the South view slavery differently?
North: many viewed slavery as wrong; South: many believed that
each state had the right to decide whether people could have
enslaved workers
How did the North and the South differ in their ideas about extending slavery?

❸ **North: did not want it to spread; South: thought people had the right**
to take enslaved workers west with them

❹ What were Northerners who wanted to do away with slavery called?
abolitionists

❺ Where did most Northerners believe slavery should not be allowed to spread?
to the western territories

(continued)

DIRECTIONS Read the paragraphs below, and then answer the questions.

Henry Clay

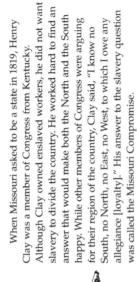

When Missouri asked to be a state in 1819, Henry Clay was a member of Congress from Kentucky. Although Clay owned enslaved workers, he did not want slavery to divide the country. He worked hard to find an answer that would make both the North and the South happy. While other members of Congress were arguing for their region of the country, Clay said, "I know no South, no North, no East, no West, to which I owe any allegiance [loyalty]." His answer to the slavery question was called the Missouri Compromise.

John Quincy Adams

John Quincy Adams, a Northerner, was the secretary of state at the time. Adams kept a diary, and in February 1820, he wrote about what he thought the future might bring. "If the dissolution [breaking apart] of the Union should result from the slave question, it is as obvious as anything . . . that it must shortly afterwards be followed by the universal emancipation [freeing] of the slaves [enslaved people] . . ."

❶ What was Henry Clay's view about the Union?
Clay thought that the Union was more important than any one
region of the country. He said he was not loyal to any one section.

❷ What did John Quincy Adams think would happen if the Union broke apart?
All enslaved people would be freed.

Name _____ Date _____

Resisting Slavery

DIRECTIONS Write the letter of the correct name or term in the space provided.

h ① Dred Scott

b ② *Freedom's Journal*

i ③ William Lloyd Garrison

i ④ Frederick Douglass

e ⑤ Sojourner Truth

g ⑥ Lucretia Mott

f ⑦ *Uncle Tom's Cabin*

c ⑧ Underground Railroad

a ⑨ Harriet Tubman

d ⑩ slave catchers

a. one of the best-known conductors of the Underground Railroad

b. the first newspaper owned and written by African Americans

c. system of secret escape routes that led enslaved people to free lands

d. a constant danger along the Underground Railroad

e. name means "traveler" of truth

f. book that told the story of how enslaved workers were mistreated

g. organized a women's rights convention in Seneca Falls, New York

h. argued that he should be free since he had once lived on free land

i. became famous for his writings and speeches against slavery

j. founded the American Anti-Slavery Society

Use after reading Chapter 12, Lesson 2, pages 482–486.   Homework and Practice Book ■ 115

Name _____ Date _____

The Nation Divides

DIRECTIONS Read the paragraphs. Then use the map below to help you answer the questions on p. 117.

The Union and the Confederacy

When Abraham Lincoln won the election of 1860, several Southern states threatened to secede from the Union. Lincoln said that he opposed secession, but he would not use military force against them. South Carolina was the first state to secede, and 10 more followed later. The states that left the Union formed their own national government called the Confederate States of America.

Soon after he was sworn in as President, the Civil War began with the battle at Fort Sumter. Most Northerners supported the Union, while most Southerners supported the Confederacy. People in the border states—Delaware, Maryland, West Virginia, Kentucky, and Missouri—were torn between the two sides. These states permitted slavery but had not seceded.

(continued)

    Use after reading Chapter 12, Lesson 3, pages 488–493.

The War Begins

DIRECTIONS In the box provided, write a brief paragraph to explain why each item on the left was important to the Civil War. Student responses will vary. Possible responses are given.

EVENT		IMPORTANT BECAUSE
Anaconda Plan	⇧	The Anaconda Plan, the Union's strategy, was to weaken the South and then invade it. Lincoln planned to blockade ports to stop the South from receiving supplies.
The Battle of Bull Run	⇧	The Battle of Bull Run, in Virginia, was the first major battle of the Civil War. The Confederates won the battle. People realized that the war would probably last a long time.
The Battle of Antietam	⇧	Neither side won a clear victory. Soon after, President Lincoln announced that he would issue an order freeing all enslaved people in areas still fighting against the Union.
The Emancipation Proclamation	⇧	It declared that all enslaved people in areas still fighting against the Union were free.

(continued)

Use after reading Chapter 12, Lesson 4, pages 498–503.

---

1 Name five of the 11 states that seceded from the Union.

Possible responses: South Carolina, Alabama, Florida, Georgia, Louisiana, Mississippi, Texas, Tennessee, Arkansas, North Carolina, Virginia

2 Which states were called the border states?

Delaware, Maryland, Kentucky, Missouri, West Virginia (1863)

3 How were border states different from other states?

These states permitted slavery but had not seceded.

4 Which state did Jefferson Davis represent in Congress before he was elected President of the Confederacy? __Mississippi__ Was it a Union or a Confederate state? __Confederate__ Write his initials in that state on the map.

5 Which state did Abraham Lincoln once represent in the United States Congress? __Illinois__ Was it a Union or a Confederate State? __Union__ Write his initials in that state on the map.

6 In which present-day state did John Brown's raid take place? __West Virginia__ Write his initials in that state on the map.

7 Where did the Civil War begin? __Fort Sumter__

8 In which state was Fort Sumter? __South Carolina__ Write "F S" in that state on the map.

9 Name the territories of the United States at the time of the Civil War.

Washington, Dakota, Nebraska, Nevada, Utah, Colorado, New Mexico, Indian Territory

Use after reading Chapter 12, Lesson 3, pages 488–493.

Skills: Distinguish Importance of Information

DIRECTIONS Read the passage below. Then read each statement that follows. If the statement is essential, write *E* in the blank. If it is incidental, write *I* in the blank.

General Robert E. Lee led the forces of the South in some of the most devastating Civil War battles. Lee was a man of such high esteem, however, that he remains loved by many Americans today. Born in Virginia in 1807, Lee was the son of a Revolutionary War hero. He ranked second in his graduating class at the United States Military Academy at West Point. Being a good soldier was important to him.

After the Civil War ended, Lee went to Richmond, Virginia. His family had lost their home and lands in Arlington, Virginia. The house had been left to Mary, Lee's wife, by her father. The Lee daughters were named Mary, Annie, Agnes, and Mildred. The oldest son was known as Custis.

Robert E. Lee later became President of Washington College in Lexington, Virginia. The school is now called Washington and Lee University. Lee died in 1870, and he is buried in Virginia. It was not until the 1970s that Lee's status as a citizen was restored. President Gerald Ford, who was born in Omaha, Nebraska, returned Lee to full citizenship.

1. **E** Robert E. Lee was an educated man of high esteem.
2. **E** Robert E. Lee's father had been a Revolutionary War hero.
3. **I** Custis was Robert and Mary Lee's oldest son.
4. **E** Washington College was renamed Washington and Lee University to honor him.
5. **I** President Gerald Ford was born in Nebraska.

DIRECTIONS Write a paragraph about how Clara Barton and other women helped the war effort.

Only men were allowed to join the army, but women found many ways to help. They took over factory, business, and farm jobs that men left behind. Some women, such as Clara Barton, worked as nurses. Barton's kindness earned her the nickname "Angel of the Battlefield." Dorothea Dix also worked as a nurse for the Union army. Sally Tompkins ran a hospital in Virginia for Confederate soldiers. Other women, such as Belle Boyd, spied for the Confederacy.

Clara Barton

Toward a Union Victory

DIRECTIONS Place the Civil War events in chronological order by numbering the events.

5 General Sherman leads the March to the Sea from Atlanta to Savannah, Georgia.

1 The Confederate army defeats a Union army at Chancellorsville.

2 The Union victory at Gettysburg marks a turning point in the war.

7 General Robert E. Lee surrenders at Appomattox Court House, Virginia.

4 Lincoln gives the Gettysburg Address.

3 Vicksburg surrenders to Union troops.

6 Confederate troops evacuate Richmond, Virginia, setting it on fire as they leave.

8 John Wilkes Booth assassinates President Lincoln.

Use after reading Chapter 12, Lesson 5, pages 506–511. **Homework and Practice Book ▪ 121**

© Harcourt

Chapter 12

Chapter Study Guide

DIRECTIONS Fill in the missing information in these paragraphs about the Civil War. Use the terms below to help you complete the paragraphs.

Lesson 1	Lesson 2	Lesson 3	Lesson 4	Lesson 5
Compromise	abolish	Abraham	emancipate	Grant
industries	Dred Scott	Lincoln	prejudice	Lee
sectionalism	Frederick	Confederacy	strategy	Meade
	Douglass	Union		

Lesson 1 The southern, northern, and western regions of the United States were very different in the 1800s. People had loyalty to their own region instead of the whole country, known as ___**sectionalism**___ . Many people who lived in the North worked in its businesses that made a product or provided a service, or ___**industries**___ . In the South, enslaved Africans worked on plantations that grew cotton and tobacco.

When Missouri asked to join the Union in 1819, it wanted to be a slave state. This would have upset the balance of free and slave states. Henry Clay came up with a solution, which became known as the Missouri ___**Compromise**___ .

Lesson 2 ___**Dred Scott**___ was an enslaved man who went to court to win his freedom. His case reached the Supreme Court. The outcome made the issue of slavery even worse for the country.

Many people worked to end, or ___**abolish**___ , slavery. ___**Frederick Douglass**___ , who had escaped from slavery, became famous for his writing and speeches against slavery.

(continued)

122 ▪ Homework and Practice Book   Use after reading Chapter 12, pages 476–513.

© Harcourt

Summarize the Chapter

⭐ Focus Skill **GENERALIZE**

DIRECTIONS Complete the graphic organizers to make generalizations about the Civil War.

Facts

| The Northern states and Southern states disagreed about slavery. | After Lincoln's election, many Southern states left the Union. | The Emancipation Proclamation expanded the goals of the war. |

Generalization

Slavery was a major issue during the nineteenth century.

Facts

| Some of Lincoln's brothers-in-law fought for the Confederacy. | Robert E. Lee knew many Civil War leaders on both sides of the conflict. | In border states, brothers, brothers and friends might fight with or even against |

Generalization

In a civil war, families and friends might fight with or even against each other.

© Harcourt

Lesson 3 Slavery was the main issue in the presidential election of 1860.

The election of **Abraham Lincoln** made some Southerners want to secede. South Carolina was the first state to secede from the **Union**. By February 1861, six more states had seceded.

Four more states seceded later. The states that left formed their own national government. It became known as the **Confederacy**.

Lesson 4 The Union's plan for winning the war was to weaken the South and then invade it. The South's **strategy** was to defend its land against Union attack.

On January 1, 1863, Lincoln issued the famous proclamation. It did not actually **emancipate** any enslaved people. Its purpose was to expand the goals of the war to include freeing all enslaved people. The South now knew that if it lost, slavery would end. This result was not acceptable to those who felt **prejudice** toward African Americans.

Lesson 5 The year 1863 saw some important victories for both armies. In May, the forces of General Robert E. **Lee** defeated a Union army at the Battle of Chancellorsville, Virginia. In July, the city of Vicksburg, Mississippi, surrendered to Union General Ulysses **Grant**. In June, Union forces, under the command of General George G. **Meade**, defeated the Confederate forces at Gettysburg after three days of fighting.

© Harcourt

Name _____ Date _____

The Last Frontier

DIRECTIONS Study the time line below. Then answer the questions that follow.

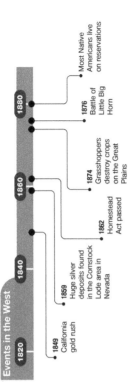

Events in the West

| 1820 | 1840 | 1860 | 1880 |

1849 California gold rush

1859 Huge silver deposits found in the Comstock Lode area in Nevada

1862 Homestead Act passed

1874 Grasshoppers destroy crops on the Great Plains

1876 Battle of Little Big Horn

Most Native Americans live on reservations

1 How many years after the California gold rush was silver found in the Comstock Lode?

10 years

2 Which two events shown on the time line directly affected settlers' lives on the Great Plains?

Homestead Act passed; Grasshoppers destroy crops on the Great Plains

3 Which event shown on the time line involved Native Americans and the United States Army?

Battle of Little Big Horn

4 How many years after the Homestead Act was passed was the Battle of Little Big Horn fought?

14 years

5 Which events shown on the time line do you think most affected the Native Americans? Explain.

Possible response: All of them. Every event pushed Native Americans off their land.

126 ■ Homework and Practice Book   Use after reading Chapter 13, Lesson 2, pages 524–529.

Name _____ Date _____

Reconstruction

DIRECTIONS Choose someone who lived during Reconstruction from the box below. Then write a letter from that person to a friend, describing what is happening in that person's life.

| A sharecropper | A new African American member of Congress |
| A white Southerner | A Northern member of Congress |

Responses will vary but should include information from the lesson showing the chosen person's point of view. A sharecropper might say that he or she is happy to be free but that sharecropping is difficult. A white Southerner might express frustration with the military government. A new African American member of Congress might be happy to be free and excited to be in Washington, working in the government. A Northern member of Congress might be frustrated with President Johnson's approach to Reconstruction.

Use after reading Chapter 13, Lesson 1, pages 516–523.   **Homework and Practice Book** ■ 125

New Industries

DIRECTIONS Read the passage below, and answer the questions that follow.

In the 1800s, the United States government made land grants to several railroad companies. More than 130 million acres were given to the Union Pacific, the Santa Fe, the Central and Southern Pacific, and the Northern Pacific railroads. In addition, western states gave the railroads 49 million acres. These land grants allowed the railroad industry to open new markets in the West for goods produced in the East.

One effect of the railroad boom was the need for stronger kinds of track. When the railroads were first built, the rails were made of iron. With the arrival of bigger and faster locomotives, however, these iron rails were not strong enough to withstand the weight of the new trains. A man named Henry Bessemer invented a way to make steel strong enough for the larger locomotives. As a result, many companies were able to ship their products throughout the United States at a faster pace.

One company that used the new, faster trains to its advantage was the Standard Oil Company. Founded by John D. Rockefeller in 1867, Standard Oil used the trains to ship oil all over the country. By 1882, Standard Oil controlled almost all of the oil refining and distribution in the United States.

1 Where did the railroad companies get the land on which they built the lines? The United States government and western states made land grants.

2 What effect did replacing iron rails with steel rails have on how United States companies could ship their products? Many United States companies could now ship their products at a faster pace.

3 What company did John D. Rockefeller found in 1867? the Standard Oil Company

4 What role do you think the railroads played in the growth of Standard Oil? Standard Oil used the railroads to ship oil all over the United States. By 1882, the company controlled most of the oil distribution in the United States.

(continued)

DIRECTIONS Write the letter of the correct description in the space provided.

1 _e_ Andrew Carnegie

2 _a_ William Jenney

3 _d_ Thomas Alva Edison

4 _c_ Alexander Graham Bell

5 _b_ Samuel Gompers

a. I built tall buildings called skyscrapers from steel.

b. I helped organize the American Federation of Labor.

c. In 1876, I invented a new model of the telephone.

d. In 1882, I set up the first electrical power station in New York City.

e. I founded the steel industry in the United States.

Name _____   Date _____

Skills: Read a Time Zone Map

DIRECTIONS Use the map below to help you answer the questions on page 130.

United States Time Zone Map

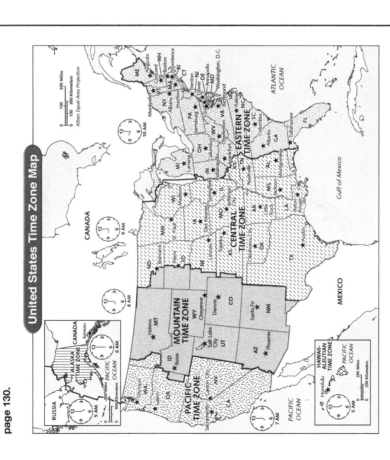

(continued)

Name _____   Date _____

1. What is the capital of California, and what time zone is it in?
   Sacramento; the Pacific time zone

2. Which two time zones cover Texas?
   the Central time zone and the Mountain time zone

3. In which time zone is the capital of Oklahoma?
   the Central time zone

4. If it is noon in the capital of Florida, what time is it in the capital of Oregon?
   9 A.M.

5. How much time difference is there between California and Hawaii?
   2 hours

6. How much time difference is there between the capital of Illinois and the capital of Colorado?
   1 hour

7. Which of these capitals is in the Eastern time zone—Indianapolis, Springfield, or Jefferson City?
   Indianapolis

8. In which time zone is the capital of New Mexico?
   the Mountain time zone

9. In which time zone is most of the Great Lakes region?
   the Eastern time zone

10. When it is 9 A.M. in the capital of Nevada, what time is it in the capital of New York?
    noon

Cities and Immigration

Early reformer Jane Addams (Chicago)

DIRECTIONS Match the choices in the first column with the descriptions.

c **1** Ellis Island

a **2** tenements

e **3** Angel Island

b **4** opposition

d **5** settlement houses

a. Many immigrants lived in these poorly-built buildings.

b. This made some people worry about new immigrants to the United States.

c. Many immigrants entered New York at this location.

d. Some reformers started these to provide food and support for new immigrants.

e. Immigrants often entered the United States at this location in San Francisco Bay.

© Harcourt

Chart and Graph Skill: Compare Different Types

DIRECTIONS Compare the graphs below to help you answer the questions on the next page.

United States Population, 1860–1900

Number of People (in thousands) — 0, 10, 20, 30, 40, 50, 60, 70, 80, 90

Year — 1860, 1870, 1880, 1890, 1900

Origin of Immigrants to the United States, 1881–1890

Europe 90.3%

The Americas 8.1%

Asia 1.3%

Other Regions 0.3%

Immigration to the United States, 1851–1900

Number of People (in thousands) — 0, 500, 1,000, 2,000, 3,000, 4,000, 5,000, 6,000

Decade — 1851–60, 1861–70, 1871–80, 1881–90, 1891–1900

(continued)

© Harcourt

Chapter 13

Chapter Study Guide

DIRECTIONS Fill in the missing information in these paragraphs about the changes and growth in the United States in the 1800s. Use the terms below to help you complete the paragraphs.

Lesson 1	Lesson 2	Lesson 3	Lesson 4
freedmen	Homesteaders	inventions	reformers
impeached	cattle	petroleum	immigrants
Reconstruction	silver	transcontinental	tenements

Lesson 1 Abraham Lincoln didn't live long enough to put his plan for **Reconstruction** into effect. The Thirteenth Amendment was ratified in 1865. It was intended to end slavery everywhere in the United States. Black codes and other practices, however, still denied rights to many citizens and **freedmen**. President Andrew Johnson took office when Lincoln died. He had many conflicts with Congress. Members of Congress **impeached** Johnson but failed to convict him.

Lesson 2 With new discoveries of gold and **silver**, many more people moved west. Ranchers raised **cattle** on the grasslands in Texas. **Homesteaders** settled on the Great Plains and started farms. Many Native Americans moved to reservations.

Use after reading Chapter 13, pages 516–547.

(continued)

---

1. Which kind of graph shows the number of immigrants who came to the United States between 1881 and 1890? **bar graph**

2. Which kind of graph shows what percentage of immigrants came from Europe in one decade? **circle graph**

3. Which kind of graph best shows change over time? **line graph**

4. How do the time periods shown on the three graphs compare? **The line graph and the bar graph cover nearly the same time period. The circle graph shows data for one decade of that time period.**

5. About how many immigrants came to the United States during the decade shown on the circle graph? Where did you find that information? **more than 5,000,000 people; on the bar graph**

6. Between which two of the years shown did the population of the United States increase the least? the most? **1860–1870; 1890–1900**

7. In which decade shown did the fewest people immigrate to the United States? **1861–1870**

8. In which decade shown did the most people immigrate to the United States? Where did most of them come from? **1881–1890; Europe**

Use after reading Chapter 13, Skill Lesson, pages 544–545.

Summarize the Chapter

⭐Focus Skill GENERALIZE

DIRECTIONS Complete the graphic organizers to make generalizations about the United States in the late 1800s and early 1900s.

Facts

Many new immigrants came to the United States.	People move west in search of wealth and opportunity.	Inventions improved travel and communication.

➡

Generalization

In the late 1880s, the United States changed a great deal because of immigration, migration, and new industries.

Facts

The railroads expanded.	Andrew Carnegie founded the United States steel industry.	Standard Oil grew to control the oil industry.

➡

Generalization

The railroads and industries grew in the late 1800s.

Use after reading Chapter 13, pages 516–547.

© Harcourt

Lesson 3 On May 10, 1869, the Union Pacific and the Central Pacific completed the nation's first **transcontinental** railroad. The spread of railroads helped people travel and helped the economy grow. At about the same time, kerosene became widely used as fuel for lamps. Its use caused the demand for and the price of **petroleum** to rise. Many **inventions**, such as the telephone and the electric lightbulb, changed how Americans lived. Many industries grew quickly at this time. People found themselves working long hours in factories. Many workers joined labor unions to protect their rights.

Lesson 4 In the late 1800s, millions of **immigrants** tried to escape violence and poverty. They did so by coming to the United States. Most of these immigrants were poor. Many lived in large cities in **tenements**. These poor apartment buildings were very crowded. For many immigrants, it was difficult to find a job. Many people feared immigrants would take their jobs, but **reformers** helped immigrants.

Use after reading Chapter 13, pages 516–547.

© Harcourt